Predicting Our Future Cyberlife:

1970-2040

Also by Nicholas Johnson

How to Talk Back to Your Television Set

Test Pattern for Living

Your Second Priority
A Former FCC Commissioner Speaks Out

Are We There Yet?
Reflections on Politics in America

Virtualosity:
Eight Students in Search of Cyberlaw

What Do You Mean and How Do You Know?
An Antidote for the Language That Does Our Thinking for Us

Predicting Our Future Cyberlife:

1970-2040

Nicholas Johnson

with

Hassan Beydoun
Wei-erh Chen
Susan Elgin
Tom Evans
Michael Fleming
Zachary Pratt
Martin Pyne
Colby Steele
Allison K. VanNatta
Sam Young

and

five anonymous authors

Lulu Press
Morrisville, North Carolina

January 2012

First Edition

ISBN: 978-1-105-62610-4

Table of Contents

Introduction

Beyond some statutory responsibilities, commissioners of the Federal Communications Commission, like other presidential appointees, can pretty much write their own job descriptions.

I served as an FCC commissioner from 1966 to 1973. To me, it then seemed somewhere between highly probable and inevitable that America was in for a communications revolution with dramatic and far-reaching consequences. It would be an electronics tsunami for which we were not only unprepared, but the very existence of which we seemed to be blissfully unaware.

So it was that my job description came to include a kind of Paul Revere role, shouting "the communications revolution is coming, the communications revolution is coming" to any and all who would listen. As my friend, and Smothers Brothers Comedy Hour head writer, Mason Williams, put it at the time, "Your problem, Nick, is that you're telling people they need to wake up, when all they want to do is sleep in late."

I encouraged foundations, think tanks, and universities' graduate programs to put personnel and money behind communications policy research. To raise public awareness, I accepted invitations for public speaking events, guest appearances on TV networks' late night shows, and radio and television stations throughout the country, wrote newspaper and magazine articles, and some 400 explanatory, often dissenting, opinions to my colleagues' FCC decisions.

And then there were the books: *How to Talk Back to Your Television Set* and *Test Pattern for Living*. (Both are now available, free, as links from the Web site, www.nicholasjohnson.org.) One of the chapters is reproduced in this book as chapter one: "Communications and the Year 2000," from *How to Talk Back to Your Television Set*. It was an attempt in 1970 to look 30 years into the future and figure out where the scarcely discernible emerging trends of 1970 might lead by 2000.

Cut to 41 years later, 2011.

One of the courses I currently teach at the University of Iowa College of Law is "Cyber and Electronic Law." One of the innovations in that course, worked out with students and law school administrators, results in the elimination of final exams–while producing more work for both students and professor. Students write a number of papers during the semester.

One of the consequences is that when the final class meeting ends, the course is over. Students have more time for their other courses–to study for finals, finish major research papers, law review or other end-of-semester obligations. However, that is not its primary purpose.

Although all the results of this experiment are not yet in, a hope (supported by some evidence) is that eliminating finals will help students focus on actually learning the material and skills they will draw upon during a 50-year career–rather than merely prepare for a single-shot exam and its resulting grade.

At least some students report that having to *use* the material throughout the semester in writing papers results in their learning more than when the focus is on an exam performance.

An inspiration for the last writing assignment this past semester (Fall 2011) was the 30-year forecast in that 1970 book chapter mentioned above, "Communications and the Year 2000." Why not have today's students think about the legal implications of where we'll be electronically 30 years from *now*? We have older students coming to law school for a career change these days, but most are recent college graduates still in their early twenties. That means that many of them were born sometime between, say, 1987 and 1990. Those revolutionary communications changes predicted in 1970, and frightening to some adults, have been the "normal" of their childhood, high school, and college years.

It would be interesting to know what this generation, having lived through the last 16 years (1995-2011), thinks we'll confront 30 years from now. Regardless of how well informed, brilliant, or prescient they may prove to be, their present judgment about their electronics future will be a major factor in shaping the law and public policy of that future.

Here was the assignment:

> Your final writing exercise is to research, think about, and write your own equivalent version [to "Communication and the Year 2000"] of a comparable exercise looking forward another 30 years: Communications in the Year 2040–with a couple of tweaks–in the . . . 2000-word range. Read Chapter 6 [of *How to Talk Back to Your Television Set*] to get a sense of what I'm proposing you do.

> What I want you to think about and address are: (a) what you think the technological innovations will be by then, (b) how they will affect our lives . . . , (c) what problems and public policy issues they will create, (d) how the law will respond (or should respond, if you believe that's different), and (e) how the practice of law will change and be impacted by these changes.

Their responses were varied and creative. However, virtually all recognized the challenges to the law of privacy posed today and intensified in the years to come.

Students were given the option to submit their paper for this book or not, and if so whether to be identified by name as the author of their paper, or as merely "Anonymous."

Here are snapshots of the papers of those authors identified by name (alphabetically, as their papers appear in the book), plus those of five who chose to be anonymous.

Hassan Beydoun fashions his view of the future from the perspective of the smartphone, the increase in its functions, and role in projecting the owner's personality–along with threats to privacy. Wei-erh Chen, as the title of his paper suggests—"Forget 'Big Brother,' The Year 2040 Will Feature The Big Family'"—sees media's continued evolution from top-down communication to a "Big Family" in which almost everyone becomes a creator as well as a consumer of media.

Susan Elgin takes a relatively optimistic view of our future, as increasing technological changes challenge the law regarding such Internet fundamentals as Net Neutrality (protected) and search engines (page rankings regulated)—with the possible exception of privacy outside the home ("non-existent"). Tom Evans envisions not only increased computer power and speed, cloud access, objects with embedded computers, and government surveillance, but the future of biological engineering, space travel, climate engineering and robotics.

Michael Fleming sees issues involving Internet governance, protecting children from obscenity, defining "property" in Internet content, the technological erosion of privacy, security (from hacking to cyber warfare), and the challenge of finding jobs for those displaced by technology. Zachary Pratt envisions more use of video in phone calls, not to mention real time holography (with the accompanying legal challenges regarding pornography), and the hacking risks once more and more home and office locks and equipment can be operated remotely from smart phones.

Martin Pyne sees a trend, likely to continue, of consolidation of control over Internet users' time (whether by force or by users' choice) by a handful of dominant firms (*e.g.*, Facebook, Google, Apple) decreasing the diversity of content and user control formerly available, while increasing the information gathered from users, especially given the increasing move to Internet access via wireless smartphones. Colby Steele's vision of 2040 is detailed, from the chip in your head, to new employment opportunities, the loss of the Fourth Amendment and enhancement of the First, to the creation of an Internet governing body, but with the ultimate conclusion that "we have lost more in privacy than we have gained in the name of safety and efficiency."

Allison VanNatta focuses on a multi-purpose embedded chip, its advantages, but more significantly the challenges it will pose for refashioning privacy law. Because its "primary purpose will be tracking everything from health data to places traveled to websites frequented," for any privacy to remain the law must evolve beyond our current "reasonable expectation of privacy" jurisprudence—to her vision of "Privacy 3.0." Finally, Sam Young projects Moore's Law (the doubling of computing power every two years) to 2040, thinks Internet access will be viewed as a basic necessity (with free or reduced prices), and sees ever-increasing threats and consequences of cyber warfare.

Anonymous 1 sees a significant increase in the breadth and depth of artificial intelligence built into handheld devices, with both its convenience for users, and privacy-eroding potential when combined with increased surveillance everywhere by law enforcement. Anonymous 2 offers a severe criticism of today's system of legal education, and sees a future in which there are but a handful of truly expert professors, while the others are relegated to the role of teaching assistants, as a higher quality online instruction is available to all, anywhere, without the necessity of significant student loans and debt.

Anonymous 3 summarizes tomorrow's technology as "smaller and connected" (such as smartphones), raising legal issues regarding providers' exploitation of users' data (requiring more transparency for users), and threats from increasingly sophisticated hackers and cyber terrorists. Anonymous 4 focuses on the changing needs for regulation, from bottom-up technology and code to top-down legislative revisions and agency enforcement. And finally, Anonymous 5 sees surveillance cameras everywhere, RFID chips embedded in all objects, including us -- a future cyber world in which we function as our own avatars, and from which we never escape.

There was a 2000-word maximum, but no endnote limits. Neither *Blue Book* nor any other formatting was required. Because the assignment involved the course casebook, references in endnotes to "Cyberlaw," "casebook," or a page number, refer to Bellia, Berman, Frischmann & Post, Cyberlaw: Problems of Policy and Jurisprudence in the Information Age (West; 4th ed., 2011).

A final note in fairness to these authors.

What is reproduced here is not intended to be a demonstration of their best efforts at a research paper. These papers reveal wider variations in the students' demonstrated writing ability, imaginative thought, legal analysis, and depth of research than would have been the case with a seminar paper. The assignment was more in the nature of a take-home exam question with a quick turn-around. Moreover, it came at the end of the semester when there were additional pressures, such as those from other courses, family obligations (some are parents), or outside employment. Thus, the primary purpose in reproducing their work is simply to offer a sampling of what this generation envisions as the technological and legal future it will be addressing in 2040.

I will not be around then to assign a revised set of grades. But if tattered copies of this book can be found at that time, by these authors or others, the accuracy of their predictions can then be measured. I am grateful to all of them for what was, for me, an enjoyable and instructive semester.

Finally, I wish to thank my assistant, Kelley Winebold, for her tireless efforts at formatting this book, my son, Gregory Johnson, for the front cover, photographer Andrea Chapman Day for the back cover photo, Dean Gail Agrawal, my University of Iowa College of Law colleagues, and my wife, Mary Vasey, for their ever-available advice and support.

–Nicholas Johnson, Iowa City, Iowa, January 2012

Chapter 1

Communications and the Year 2000 (1970)(

Nicholas Johnson

Communication touches every fiber of our lives. The American communications mosaic includes a Defense Department hot line, a child tranquilized before a TV set, a ringing telephone, a politician campaigning by radio, a news service teletype, a fog-bound ship's radar, a hidden microphone in a business meeting, satellites, and computerized airline reservations.

When we speak of communications we often forget the social science implications of these technological achievements. How do they relate to all the other major characteristics and problems of our time (war, overpopulation, increased leisure, congested cities, mounting popular unrest)? How do they affect the life of an individual--in an industrialized modern city, or in a remote rural village? How do they affect the creation and exercise of political power? How do they affect relations between family members -- and nations? To understand where communications technology is taking us, we need more than the insights of economists and engineers. I think we need the vision of anthropologists, sociologists, psychologists, educators, political scientists, general semanticists -- and a poet or two.

I like to talk about trends rather than explosions or revolutions because they can be more easily seen, believed, and dealt with. Here are a couple of examples of what I mean. Before the transistor was invented it is unlikely that anyone, outside of a few scientists experimenting with the possibility, would have predicted it. Even then, however, one could detect a trend toward smaller and smaller vacuum tubes. Before the launch capability existed, few would have predicted the operation of space communications satellites. Now that the satellites are operational, however, it is easy to detect the trends toward greater satellite power, longer life, increased channel capacity, and precision of transmission beam. In short, I do not think it is useful for a layman to try to predict the wholly new transmission scheme that will be to the 1990's what the satellite has been to the 1960's. (How close could the communications system of 1969 have been predicted in 1938?) I do think it is useful to try to reflect upon the trends that are already visible.

The most significant trend in communications today is probably the trend toward instantaneous, ubiquitous, no-cost access to all information. I do not for a moment suggest that we are going to reach that destination; I only suggest that what is happening today, and will likely continue for thirty years, can most easily be understood by navigating with that landmark on the far horizon. If we are

---

* As explained in the Introduction, this material was written in 1970 and published as Chapter 6 in Nicholas Johnson, *How to Talk Back to Your Television Set* (Little, Brown, 1970), pp. 131-147.

0.01 percent of the way there by 1970, we may be 15 percent of the way there by the year 2000 -- for we must also deal with a trend of acceleration in the rate of change. Now what do I mean by "instantaneous, ubiquitous, no-cost access to all information"?

First, "instantaneous." Not only can we now communicate faster than we used to--via telephone, telegraph, television -- but communications channels (in cables and satellites) are capable of moving increasingly more information, and thus more information per unit time. Computers process information faster than ever and are being coupled with communications networks. This is not a revolution, it is a trend that has existed throughout the history of man. It's going on now, and will continue. The only thing that is changing is the rate of acceleration in the speed of transmission. We will not reach literal instantaneity by the year 2000. There are many delays in the system, and the ultimate barrier of 186,000 miles per second shows no signs of crumbling. But that at least seems to be the direction of our journey.

By "ubiquitous" I simply mean that the number of points of access to a communications network are continuing to increase at an accelerated rate, even to the point of being personally mobile. You are never very far from a telephone instrument in the United States, and more are being installed every day. The ease of use of the system, even on a worldwide basis, and the increasing amount of information that can be obtained by telephone, is interacting with the increasing number of instruments to accelerate the trend. The Bell System's touch tone push-button sets, the direct distance dialing, and the relatively short period (approximately thirty seconds) that is needed to reach another phone produce increased telephone usage. The international telephone system is developing similar improvements. (These factors are also, of course, related to instantaneity.) More information can be accessed by telephone: library research desks, time and weather reports, stock market reports, and, of course, the data-phone interconnecttion of computers with the rapid increase in number, character and simplicity of terminal devices for home and office. Personally portable mobile communication devices are likewise increasing. Communication on ships and airplanes is common. There is an increasing number of mobile land vehicles with communications facilities, from earth moving equipment and fork lift trucks in warehouses to police cars and taxicabs. Mobile individuals are equipped with two-way radio equipment or paging devices on their person. Mobile teleprinters and computer access are just beginning what will probably be a trend that will include other terminal devices. The instruments of mass communication are undergoing the same trends. Television and radio sets are spreading throughout the world. The pocket transistor radio makes personally mobile mass communications possible everywhere, and the number of portable television sets is also increasing.

I do not predict a day of free communications. I do believe, however, that we can identify a trend of decreasing cost of communications that is likely to continue. This is, in part, the result of an accelerating and interlocked relationship between miniaturization, mass production and distribution, and reduced cost. Earthbound microwave relay towers can provide transmission facilities at about one percent of the cost of open wire circuits. Satellites are even cheaper for long haul traffic. The capacity of laser beams is reported to be so enormous that it is almost impossible even to compute the low cost of providing a circuit. Television and radio receiving sets continue to come down in price. Furthermore, it is important to distinguish between cost and price. Obviously, the sum total of prices paid for communications service must equal the sum total of the costs of providing that service plus a profit. But that does not tell you anything about either the costs to be allocated to a given service, or the pricing system that will be used to regain those costs. Example: the U.S. Congress has provided that the FCC may authorize free interconnection of the educational television stations in the United States. As we do that, it will not mean there will be no cost to the telephone company associated with providing this service; it will mean there is no price to the educational broadcasters. To the extent the service requires the telephone company to incur additional costs they will be absorbed by the prices charged for other services. Another example: local service and WATS (wide area telephone service). Within most local exchanges the costs of telephone service are assessed on a system-wide basis, and the prices charged are on a flat-fee-for-unlimited-use basis. WATS is a similar pricing scheme for "long distance" calls: for a flat fee a subscriber may make an unlimited number of calls within a defined area outside of his local exchange. Under such pricing schemes there is no additional cost to the user for using the service. He will make an economic judgment in deciding whether to get the service at all; once he gets it, however, he will use it without regard to economic judgments. Note that such pricing schemes have the same effect upon communications behavior as if they were technological innovations that made communications equipment and service available "free."

It is, of course, fanciful to suggest that by the year 2000--or any other year for that matter -- we will have a world in which every human being will [126] have access literally to "all" information. Like the other end points on our present trend lines, however, it seems a useful concept. Even today, anyone who can pay the subscription rates, or can use a major library, has access to--if not all information--at least considerably more information than he wants or can possibly use. The world's professional people are already at the point where they really have more desire for services that will edit, summarize, process, and retrieve relevant information than for services that merely give them access to more data. Yet that is really more an emotional judgment born of frustration than a rational preference. We need both. In any event, we have little choice we are going to have access to more information with which to do our jobs whether we want it or not. The number of telephones that can be reached from any other telephone is increasing every year--a function of the increase in the absolute number of telephones and in the number of units that are interconnected. With an increase in research activity, publishing, leisure time, levels of education, and disposable income, the absolute amount of information, and the number of people who will want it, is multiplying rapidly. We have increased the number and sensitivity of apparatus for recording various phenomena. The computer continues to increase our capacity to receive, process and use this data. The international exchange of printed matter and films is today being augmented by television.

The program One World in 1967 was an immensely successful effort to interconnect television cameras around the world, via satellite, to TV stations which broadcast to an international audience made up of the largest number of viewers ever to watch simultaneously a single program or performance. The widespread coverage of the moon walk achieved similar ratings. I suspect we will share more such experiences. As computers take on the data retrieval tasks now done by laborious manual library searches, whole new worlds of information will be opened up to more widespread use. There is no reason video and audio tape libraries couldn't be made similarly accessible--and all of them from remote points if desired. (This is not to suggest the demise of pre-programmed "network" television offerings--there is the same desire for video information packaging as for print -- only that the individual's opportunities for individual choice will expand.) So we are rapidly approaching the time--if we have not already passed it--when the principal impediments to "access to all information" will not be technological imperfections, the availability of circuits, or price, but the man-made inhibitions: copyright, proprietary business data, national security classifications, ignorance, inertia, and stubbornness.

Perhaps the single most important implication of "communications and the year 2000" is the extent to which it will be something which we have planned for, designed and built, rather than predicted. The space program will be found to have had its greatest impact, in my view, in philosophy and psychology--not new technology and scientific data. The greatest inhibitions to man's progress and happiness are those of his own making: "it's scientifically impossible," "we can't afford it," "but that would be socialistic," "it's illegal," "it's against our policy," "our church doesn't believe in that," "it's just not done that way." To remove these shackles from our minds required the preposterously expensive program necessary to get us to the moon. Now that we have done it we are beginning to change the way we talk about our opportunities: "if we can send a man to the moon we can certainly do . . ." has become the opening line of some very imaginative proposals. Political philosophy has become hopelessly confused and almost irrelevant in the frantic search for pragmatic solutions to common problems: the "socialist bureaucrats in Washington" are trying to sell their Post Office Department to the highest bidder in the marketplace; the "rugged individualists" of American business who cuss the "fuzzy-headed do-gooder liberals" are now profiting as government contractors in city building, job training and America's fifty-two-billion- dollar education industry, and are coming up with very humane proposals after sitting on commissions and task forces on civil disorders, employment, crime, and violence. Barry Goldwater's "conservative" economist, Dr. Milton Friedman, has proposed a guaranteed annual income ("negative income tax,') as an alternative to welfare; it is a proposal that, in an earlier day, would have been rejected out of hand because of its "communist" origins ("from each according to his ability, to each according to his need").

Books like Brave New World and 1984 and much of our current writing have stressed the oppressive potential of "instantaneous, ubiquitous, no-cost access to all information." There was even substantial public protest when the telephone company in the United States wanted to take the "dehumanizing" step of abolishing the exchange names from the telephone numbers (that is, substituting 395-4321 for EXecutive 5-4321). Students at Berkeley have carried picket signs saying, "I am a person. Do not bend, fold, spindle or mutilate," as a protest to the faceless machines that require cards carrying such instructions. For every one person who sees advantage to a national databank (for example, to more efficiently match job opportunity to available workers), there are a dozen who fear its power, and the impossibility of clearing error from one's record. The efficiency of automatic video tape recorders in filming auto accidents, and closed circuit television systems in doing the work of guards, must be balanced against the very understandable human protest at such "invasions of privacy." The wonders of powerful, miniaturized microphones and transmitters have already succeeded in severely limiting the places where one may confidently carry on a "private" conversation. Fears of wiretapping have substantially impeded the telephone system as a communications network.

We have moved from an age when political and economic power were measured in land, or capital, or labor, to an age in which power is measured largely by access to information and people. The man or institution which has the greatest political, military or economic power today is the one with access to the greatest amount of relevant information in the most usable form in the quickest time; and, in institutions or societies where popular understanding and support are relevant, the greatest access to the mass media. Thus, the problem in creating national or international satellite-direct-to-home radio and television is not technological; it is getting those who now control the mass media to agree on the individuals and procedures that will determine what is broadcast over that satellite channel. The problem in establishing cable television throughout the U.S. is not that of deciding where we will put all those wires; it is deciding who gets to hold the switch. The argument is being advanced that the mass media should be more like a common carrier; that the First Amendment guarantees of free speech must, today, extend to making the mass media available to those who want to use them. As cable television and laser beams replace an economy and technology of scarcity with one of abundance, that will be increasingly possible technologically. Whether it will be socially and politically possible remains to be seen.

I recall a conversation with representatives from fire and police departments in one of America's largest cities. Why, I asked, did they not establish mobile radio systems that would enable fire, police and national guardsmen at the scene of a particular incident to talk to each other? After some stumbling around the answer became quite clear: each wanted to retain power and control in his own organization. Within any paper-shuffling bureaucracy (corporate or government) power lies with he who controls the key to the filing cabinet. To make information that is now someone's personal domain easily accessible threatens his status and prestige -- perhaps the justification for his job. Government agencies could very easily put their "public" information in computers that could be operated by any member of the public. They probably will not do so--but not because "it's scientifically impossible," or "it costs too much." The education establishment has been very slow to accept educational television--it has been viewed as a threat by many classroom teachers. They are unlikely to welcome with any greater enthusiasm programmed-instruction teaching machines in the home that any member of the family can use to study any subject of his choosing at his leisure. As former Secretary of Defense McNamara demonstrated at the Defense Department, the "management information system" lies at the heart of management's power over any large organization today. If access to that information is diffused, so is power. That is the reason--not economic or technical feasibility--it is unlikely there will be more than a handful of visual display terminals with access to management information data in any large organization.

We are witnessing on all sides today a revolution of "participatory democracy." The people want, as we say, a "piece of the action." Every candidate for President in 1968 advocated this concept in some form. It finds its philosophical counterpart in most of the civilized nations of the world today. It is, in my judgment, a function of increased communications, education and standard of living. Nation states grow obsolete, mass-appeal political leaders vanish, and the mass media in effect become government, as education is substituted for mass illiteracy, popular access to the mass media is substituted for dictatorial control over information by a single leader, identity and loyalty to one's institutional and professional affiliations are substituted for geographical relationships, and internationally understood professional languages are substituted for national languages and literature. I think those trends will accelerate before they slow down. No segment of the various movements of social protest has a very specific program at this point. But it is only a matter of time before they grasp the "information-is-power" concept even more fully.

We have already reached the point where the educational-social-economic-professional elites of Tokyo, London, Moscow, Washington, New York, and so forth, have much more in common with one another than they have in common with their own countrymen back in the rural villages. This is yet another trend. And the number being influenced by it is expanding geographically and economically. Trade, transportation and--especially--communication is the principal reason. The same music, television shows, and movies are seen and heard around the world. Every country loses a little of its individual character as it undergoes this process. Americans are concerned about the possible relation between violence in television shows and violence in our streets. But this is a matter of international concern as well, because these television shows are shown around the world. Finland, Spain and some other countries have taken action to prohibit the importation of some American television. But most countries have not, and the U.S. government makes no effort, so far as I know, to exert any control over the content, and possible impact, of our exported television product.

One of the principles to which America is dedicated, as an ideal, is that every individual should have the opportunity to attain the maximum growth and development of which he is capable. This is a revolutionary philosophy, impossible of complete attainment, and it has created considerable grief for our country, especially during the past few years. But we keep striving to come closer to this ideal each year, and we are as proud of our progress as we are determined to make up the remaining gap. It is why we must make available at no cost recreational facilities to develop the body, schools and libraries to develop the mind, and churches and national parks to develop the spirit.

Our progress toward "instantaneous, ubiquitous, no-cost access to all information" has important implications for our commitment to individual opportunity. President Johnson's last nomination to the FCC was Mr. H. Rex Lee, who, as a distinguished and imaginative Governor of Samoa, established an educational television system for the islands that has shown the world what our new communications techniques can mean in improving the quantity and quality of education while reducing its cost. At a time when the rate of illiteracy in the world is increasing rather than decreasing with every passing year it is obvious that some dramatic changes in educational techniques are called for. Governor Lee's electronic schoolhouse may suggest a way. And I would remind you once again in this context that we can make the informational resources of the world available "free" to the user if we choose to do so. We are not just playing with public-utility-ratemaking metaphysics when we set telephone rates --we are affecting the individual opportunity of the world's people.

On signing the Public Broadcasting Corporation bill into law, President Johnson said, "Today our problem is not making miracles--but managing them." The space program has impressed upon us the realization that we have the human talent and economic resources to do anything worth doing if we are fully committed to its achievement. This realization substantially alters the task of the planner or forecaster. His task is no longer merely one of predicting technological and economic phenomena. He must call upon the resources of social scientists, philosophers and poets to assist him in his search for a set of values, or the goals that he seeks to achieve. For we are in the enviable if anomalous position of having capabilities that exceed our aspirations. Whether we know it or not we are making decisions today that will determine, irrevocably, the impact of communications upon our society and economy in the year 2000.

Each technological innovation in communications raises a number of questions. What will be its impact on our society? How can this new force most effectively be channeled to human good? Are unrestrained market forces or some form of government regulation most appropriate? Are new or amended laws or regulations necessary? What is the most economic and efficient way to achieve the ends sought? What are the forces regulating the development and rate of introduction of the new technology? Are they effective in serving interests beyond private economic gain? How can government be most effectively structured and administered to deal with the problem in question? What additional data, analysis, or other research is called for? Whether we make wise decisions, whether we mold our future intentionally, is up to us.

What will be the state of communications in the year 2000? Largely whatever we choose to make it. Of course, we must do more than simply utter the phrase, "The future is what we make of it." There is a limit to the capacity of human society to preplan its course of evolution, and even some question about the desirability of doing so. Our under taking here, and in those other countries with Commissions on the Year 2000, is motivated in part by our fascination with the advent of a new century. But we are also cognizant of the increasing desire on the part of post-industrial societies to prevent impersonal and unforeseen chance to force our society's evolution. At the same time we acknowledge that the natural forces in a market economy often have the capacity to achieve the goals that a society has set for itself. So what do we do? First, we should exert every effort to maintain and improve open societies, where conflicting information, interpretations and orthodoxies have an opportunity to be heard and tested. For we have an ultimate commitment to the ideal that a society must choose, through some form of the democratic process, what course it wants to follow. That choice is made more meaningful, especially in times of rapid change, when the alternatives are made clear and their implications have been fully enunciated. Secondly, we should endeavor to test all the change which is so surely to be part of the years ahead. I would hope that the next three decades would be known for our experimentation and pilot projects on a grand scale. And when we test, we will try to develop better standards for measuring the achievement of the human values so long cherished by all mankind.

---

[1] For example, a smart phone can now be used to remote control a surveillance device, such as a small helicopter with a camera attached to it.

Chapter 2

The Rise of the Smartphone
Hassan Beydoun

I.   Introduction and Overview

If you asked someone half a century ago what technological innovations they thought would exist in 2011, chances are you would hear things about flying cars or jet-packs. Industries like transportation dominated the thoughts of consumers and engineers alike then. Many innovations were ahead of their time and primarily of conceptual importance. But times have changed. We are now a post-industrial society focused on communication. In this Digital Age, technological innovations respond to our growing need to quickly access information and increase productivity. The days of "conceptual importance" are fading away. It now seems as though every innovation has a direct practical consequence on both society and the law. Simply put, the implications of technological change are more important now than they have ever been.

Consequently, one must ask: will there be a similar revolution over the next 30 years? Because there is still much capacity and demand for innovation in the field of communications, it is likely that technological change through 2040 will instead be an evolution. I believe that the most important change driving this evolution will be the further advancement of the smartphone over other technologies, such as the PC. This belief consists of two related predictions, one aimed at the aggregate effects of future smartphone advancements and the other at the individual effects. After fully positing these predictions, I will discuss the societal and legal implications of this technological change, as well as its effect on the practice of law.

II.   Predictions of Technological Change Through 2040

The smartphone has transitioned from a hobby of early adopters, to one of the most important products of our day-to-day lives. Many of us check email, make calls, surf the internet, shop online, take pictures, do online banking, play games, and enjoy music and movies, all from our smartphones. It is a technology that truly puts the informational universe at your fingertips. Additionally, its application seems to be limitless, as new technologies and capabilities are constantly being utilized.[1] Given how rapidly phones have developed within the past decade alone, it would be difficult to predict the smartphone of 2040. Notwithstanding that uncertainty, it is almost guaranteed that two predictions will prove true by that time: 1) the ubiquitous presence and utilization of smartphones; and 2) the smartphone will become an extension of its owner's identity and person. The first prediction reflects the aggregate effect that future smartphone technology will have, while the latter reflects the effects on an individual.

A. The Ubiquitous Presence and Utilization of Smart Phones

Currently, about 30% of phone subscribers use a smartphone.[2] I believe that this number, as well as the number of total subscribers, will grow exponentially by 2040. Smartphones will increasingly affect the way we live as new applications for it are found. It makes sense that something we always keep in our pockets would be the best candidate to use for bringing technology into various aspects of our lives.[3] Conversely, the more ways we find to increase our productivity using a smartphone, the more important it is to always keep on us. This endless circle will ensure that the smartphone will overshadow all other consumer technologies in 30 years.

This is supported by the current and massive migration of cell-phone users towards smartphones. As smartphones are increasingly adopted, more service providers will cater to these users. In turn, more smartphone users will rely on the technology as a convenient means to productivity and more people will want to adopt the new technology for that same purpose.[4] Such methods in achieving near-universal adoption are not unprecedented. The PC started off similarly and became the most important device we use. Although some tasks are best suited for a PC, a smartphone could do what a PC can and much more.[5] Because of the convenience[6] and wider range of smartphone applications, it will be in the future what the PC is today, while likely becoming even more ubiquitous.

As smartphones move towards this ubiquitous presence, we will increasingly rely on them as a primary channel to the digital world.[7] This increased reliance means that these devices will contain increasingly valuable personal data. Our financial information,[8] calls, messages, pictures, etc., will all be stored on our phone. The more we utilize smart phones to their full potential, the more important and valuable the data stored on them is.

B.   Smart Phones as an Extension of One's Identity and Person

Two smartphone technologies to be heavily utilized in the future will help demonstrate its effect on our individual lives: 1) Near-field communication technology (NFC); and 2) location-based services (LBS). Because of its versatile nature, in addition to these advancements, the smartphone will become an extension of our identity and person.

NFC chips are used by programs like Google-Wallet and allow phones to communicate with devices in close proximity. This would allow payment for items at cash registers by waiving one's phone. NFC chips could also transform a phone into an ID card, which could be used to regulate authorized access to places and things. In essence, NFC technology would transform the smartphone into a digital replacement for the wallet.[9]

In contrast, GPS chips primarily drive LBS.[10] The effects LBS have on individuals are as varied as its applications: it allows for location broadcasting on social networks, as well as turn-by-turn navigation. Even the online-dating industry has begun to realize its potential.[11] Perhaps most importantly, LBS would allow tracking of individuals.[12] Furthermore, the global market for LBS is projected to double by only 2016.[13]

The versatile nature of the smartphone is such that it will aid us in many aspects of life.[14] By utilizing NFC and LBS, developers will finally begin to maximize the potential of smartphones. As more services are catered to smartphones, more people will adopt and rely on the technology. Accordingly, the future smartphone will contain our most personal data, data that on its own would paint a comprehensive picture of its user's identity.[15] NFC and LBS will play a significant part in this personification of the smartphone because both involve such personal data. Accordingly, I predict that in 2040 the advancement of the smart phone will result in it becoming an extension of its user's identity, as well as that person's representative in the digital universe.

III.   The Legal and Societal Issues Arising From Smart Phone Advances in 2040

At this point it has been argued that by 2040 one of the most important technological advances will be the exponential growth of the smartphone. Specifically, the smartphone will be fully utilized to become an extension of an individual's identity and will have a ubiquitous presence in society, as well as in each of our lives. This raises an important public policy concern with respect to privacy, as future smartphones will hold extensive personal data. Arising from this concern are two significant issues the law must address: 1) how could smartphone users legally be protected against hacking and malware; 2) smartphone privacy concerns under the Fourth Amendment. Following an analysis of these issues, I will touch on this technology's impact on the practice of law.

A.   Smartphone Hacking, Malware, and the CFAA

Smartphones are prime targets for hacking and malware.[16] Given my two predictions, the importance of this risk will be greatly amplified by 2040. Computers are protected against this risk by the Computer Fraud and Abuse Act (CFAA). Thus, the question is whether the CFAA's protections also extend to smartphones. Congress has previously amended the CFAA to widen the scope of the definition of "computers."[17] The CFAA provides that "an electronic . . . or other high-speed data processing device performing logical functions," is a computer.[18]

This broad definition should include smartphones, which have processors that are more powerful than some PCs.[19] This interpretation of the CFAA was very recently agreed with by the 8th Circuit, which held that a relatively weak processor in a Motorola flip-phone made it fall within the CFAA's "computer" definition.[20] Two Senators have even recently requested that the Department of Justice interpret the CFAA in accordance with the 8th Circuit's ruling.[21] Consequently, the CFAA would protect smartphones against malware and hacking.

B. Smartphone Privacy Concerns and the Fourth Amendment

My second prediction was that smartphones would become an extension of their user's identity partly due to the extensive personal data they store. This raises a legitimate privacy concern and the subsequent issue of whether police may search one's phone without a warrant under the Fourth Amendment. This issue is especially important given the Supreme Court's decision in Atwater v. Lago Vista, which upheld the validity of the arrest of a woman pulled over for only a minor traffic stop.[22] Thus, if the law allows warrantless searches of smartphones incident to an arrest for something as minor as a traffic violation, a truly scary precedent will be set that ignores our present conception of privacy. Current law allows police to search any "container" near a person without a warrant if incident to that person's arrest.[23] Some courts have upheld the search of a cell-phone's content incident to arrest and without a warrant under the theory that it is a "container" similar to an address book, as it stores numbers.[24] But how will courts respond in applying old precedents to advancing smartphone technology where extensive personal data is at stake, not simply phone numbers? How should the legal rule adjust to this technological change?

One state has already ruled on the issue. In State v. Smith, the Ohio Supreme Court held that the search of a defendant's cell phone violated the Fourth Amendment due to the smartphone's ability to hold large amounts of diverse personal information.[25] Modern phones do not resemble the "containers" that older phones were classified under for Fourth Amendment purposes. The heightened interest of privacy with respect to smartphones outweighed any arguments in the government's favor. I believe other courts, including the U.S. Supreme Court, should and will eventually follow Ohio's lead in holding that smartphones are distinct from "containers" under the Fourth Amendment and are thus protected from warrantless searches. Such an adjustment to an existing legal rule based on technological change would not be unprecedented, as such occurred with wiretapping when Katz v. U.S. overruled Olmstead v. U.S.[26]

C. The Effect on the Practice of Law

Perhaps the most important consequence of smartphone advances on the practice of law itself will be on e-discovery in civil litigation. With the advent of email and computers, e-discovery became a major part of corporate litigation. Because of my predictions above, the smartphone is likely to introduce a much greater risk for company compliance with e-discovery efforts if mobile data becomes subject to discovery guidelines.[27] The following article summed up this e-discovery issue well:

The introduction of [smartphones] has made many companies' e-discovery strategies obsolete; corporations are unable to keep pace with the increasingly common view of the courts that new technology innovations are fair game in the eyes of the law and subject to the rules of discovery. . . . Failing to [address this issue] can be disastrous – resulting in inadmissible evidence, court sanctions and even courtroom losses. This is particularly true as the courts show that while they understand the challenges associated with e-discovery, they are increasing reticent to overlook errors and accept an "honest mistake" defense.[28]

Consequently, attorneys must be more active in advising their clients on mobile policy to ensure such risks are mitigated, especially as more companies supply their employees with increasingly versatile smartphones. Attorneys representing small and large companies will thus be required to maintain a working knowledge of IT services in order to properly advise their clients. Conversely, attorneys on the plaintiff's side of a civil suit must also acknowledge that smartphones, in addition to computers, may contain relevant information and, if so, should be requested for discovery. Most importantly, attorneys should advise their clients that if e-discovery software can access a smartphone, so can the "bad guys," and thus should advise their client on mobile use policy accordingly.

---

[2] Blake Ellis, *Your Smart Phone Could be Your Most Dangerous Possession*, CNN Money (January 11, 2011) *available at*
http://money.cnn.com/2011/01/11/pf/smartphone_dangers/index.htm
[3] "[Smartphones] are extremely personal devices which people tend to always have within reach and most often switched on. This enables opportunities which other channels lack," says Telecom Analyst Richard Anderson, Berg Insight, *available at* http://www.berginsight.com/News.aspx?m_m=6&s_m=1
[4] A good example of this is mobile banking. A recent research report by Berg Insight predicts that the number of mobile banking users will increase from the 133 million users at present, to over 709 million users by 2015. Moreover, "in developing regions such as Africa, the mobile phone will become the primary digital channel for people to conduct financial services in the coming years." *Available at*
http://www.berginsight.com/News.aspx?m_m=6&s_m=1
[5] For example, the ability to tap into a mobile telecommunications network is a very significant advantage for smart phones over computers. Computers may be connected to such a network via a broadband card, but the extra cost and required hardware make the use of a smart phone much more convenient. Smart phones are also much more mobile than even the lightest laptop and can be away from its charger for a considerably longer period.
[6] There is much to be said about the convenience of the smart phone. It is always close to you, since it is used as a primary communications device for so many people, and so is the most readily available means of staying connected to the digital world we live in. Also, because it is a primary and (arguably) necessary device to carry around, consumers can replace many other gadgets they have by purchasing a multi-functional smartphone.
[7] See note 3, supra.
[8] The widespread adoption of NFC technology, discussed *infra*, means that people will have credit card information stored in their phone. Online banking may result in account information being stored, especially with the use of banking apps. Online shopping may also result in account information being stored on a phone.

[9] Just as many have stopped carrying cash because of the convenience and benefits of credit cards, many will use their phone as a digital wallet to pay for goods.

[10] Triangulating a phone's Wi-Fi signal can also drive LBS, but this method is less reliable and precise than GPS.

[11] Leena Rao, *OKCupid Integrates Location Based Dating Into iOS and Android Apps*, Tech Crunch (August 11, 2011). *Available at* http://techcrunch.com/2011/08/11/okcupid-integrates-location-based-dating-into-ios-and-android-apps/

[12] See, e.g., Sprint's Family Locator, which allows parents to supply their child with a GPS smartphone and monitor their location via an online map, *available at* https://sfl.sprintpcs.com/finder-sprint-family/

[13] According to a new market report from the Berg Insight firm, annual revenues for LBS are projected to grow from about € 150 to € 300 million by 2016. *Available at* http://www.berginsight.com/News.aspx?m_m=6&s_m=1

[14] For example, it helps us do our banking, it entertains us, it provides us with access to the world of digital content, etc.

[15] The smartphone will contain all the information that makes one so unique: the people you talk to, shopping habits, financial information, where you go, what you do, etc.

[16] Many authors have declared 2012 the year of "mobile malware." In the past four months alone malware on the Android OS has increased 427%. See Dan Tynan, *Mobile Malware Epidemic*, PC World (Nov. 20, 2011) *available at* http://www.pcworld.com/article/244346/mobile_malware_epidemic_looms.html

[17] Casebook at p.733.

[18] *Id.*

[19] Indeed, HTC is now in the process of releasing a quad-core smartphone, the Zeta, while most computers only have a dual core processor.

[20] *U.S. v. Kramer*, 631 F.3d 900 (8th Cir. 2011).

[21] Gautham Nagesh, *Senators say digital privacy law covers smartphones*, The Hill (April 13, 2011) *available at* http://thehill.com/blogs/hillicon-valley/technology/155795-senators-say-digital-privacy-law-covers-smartphones

[22] 532 U.S. 318 (2001). The woman in this case was pulled over for failure to wear a seat belt while returning from her kids' soccer practice.

[23] See *New York v. Belton*, 453 U.S. 454 (1981).

[24] In *U.S. v. Curtis*, the 5th Circuit upheld the search of a man's text messages used to charge him with mortgage fraud, when that search was incident to an unrelated arrest. No. 09-2049 (5th Circuit Court of Appeals, 2011).

[25] 920 N.E.2d 949 (2009).

[26] Casebook at p.306-309.

[27] This is because the smartphone will handle extreme amounts of data as we rely on them more and as they reach a ubiquitous presence.

[28] Jeff Fehrman, *Mobile Devices: A Singular Threat to Corporate Compliance and E-Discovery*, Corporate Compliance Insights (January 4, 2011) *available at* http://www.corporatecomplianceinsights.com/2011/mobile-devices-a-singular-threat-to-corporate-compliance-and-e-discovery.

Chapter 3

Forget "Big Brother;" 2040 Will Feature the "Big Family"

Wei-erh Chen

I.   Introduction

In 1970, then FCC commissioner Nicholas Johnson wrote "Communications and the Year 2000," wherein Johnson sought to imagine the state of communications at the turn of the new millennium.[1] To do this, Johnson extrapolated from "the trends that are already visible" and proposed that communications would move "toward instantaneous, ubiquitous, no-cost access to all information."[2] Now in 2011, this essay will follow in the spirit of Johnson's article and suggest one possible vision of the state of technology in the year 2040.

This essay proposes that over the next thirty years, traditional mass media will be increasingly supplanted by an internet-driven and social media-based model of communication that will collapse many of the distinctions between producers, consumers, and regulators of communicated content. To support this claim, this essay will first identify the visible present-day trends that may lead to a radical restructuring of society's major channels of communication. Second, this essay will unpack how the rise of social media-based communication may affect those in the year 2040. Next, this essay will consider some public policy issues arising from this technology. Finally, this essay will explore some possible responses to these emerging problems.

II.   Contemporary Trends in Online and Mass Media

The mass media industry in the last century was characterized by a highly centralized system where different participants played distinct and generally non-overlapping roles.[3] There were three main groups in this system: content creators, content consumers, and content regulators.[4] Content creators, such as the local and national broadcasters, record labels, and film and television studios, were a relatively small number of businesses that controlled the means of producing and distributing content for widespread consumption.[5] Content consumers, on the other hand, were the many members of the general public who tuned in to the producers' content but had little ability to transmit any of their own original content. Finally, content regulators such as the FCC developed as a regulatory agency designed to oversee the content creators' actions.[6] While these groups traditionally fulfilled separate and distinct functions within the communications system, that type of compartmentalization is now giving way as the rise of social and online media reinvents the roles of all three groups.

The trend over the last decade has been a dramatic increase in a consumer's ability to engage and respond to social and content media with a world-wide community in real time.[7] This new-found ability represents a significant departure from the traditional system in at least three ways. First, the consumer has gained the ability to directly discuss the content with both the content creator and other third parties.[8] Second, the consumer is no longer limited to discussing the content with those whom she interacts with in real life, but may engage with complete strangers around the world in real time during an actual program or event.[9] Lastly, social media allows content consumers to become content creators and broadcasters themselves by responding to and expanding upon the content they have received.[10]

Given this emerging trend in social and mass media, the year 2040 would conceivably be populated by a "Big Family," where a large and decentralized community of individuals, groups, and corporations have a broad ability to simultaneously monitor, consume, discuss, and produce media for online distribution. In contrast to a future where a single "Big Brother" is the Panopticon whose invasiveness keeps citizens in line, the "Big Family" would be characterized by a willingness to share one's life with many other persons, and in turn, engage with those other lives just as members of a traditional family would be. These bonds, of course, may not be as permanent as the bonds built within a nuclear family, but the content and information that may be provided could be even more intimate or personal than that which is shared with the traditional family. In this way, the traditional model for mass media, where communications largely flows in one direction from the broadcaster to the consumer[11] will give way to communications in the "Big Family" era where conversations will likely become a cacophony of unique, targeted, and personalized conversations among many different parties (See figure 1).[12]

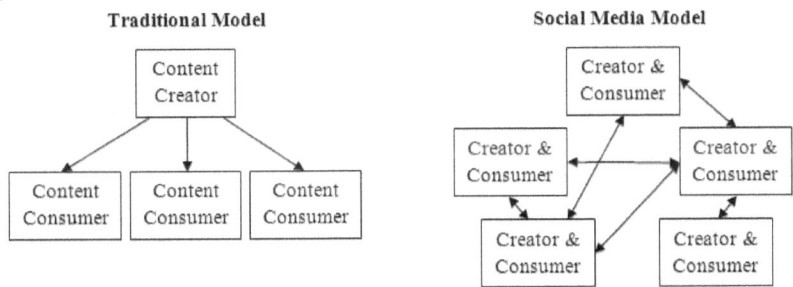

Figure 1: Contrasting the Traditional and Social Media Models.[13]

III.   The "Big Family's" Effects on Society in 2040

The emergence of social media driven content and communication will have a wide-ranging effect on many areas of society in 2040. This essay will address the "Big Family's" impact on four of these areas—business, media, privacy, and the legal industry.[14]

A. Business

Traditionally, if a business wanted customer feedback on a certain product or service, the business would need to be proactive in eliciting such information from its customers.[15] The current trend, however, is toward a more organic and continuous dialogue between the business and its customers. For example, companies such as Coca-Cola and Eastman Kodak have created Social Media Policies for interacting with clients online.[16] Coca-Cola has designed a certification program to train official online spokespersons and implemented principles to guide the spokespersons' online interactions[17], while Kodak has, among other actions, hired a "Chief Listener" to monitor online conversations directed at or related to the company.[18] For the first time in history, continuous consumer input is regularly influencing business decisions.[19] Following this trend, it may become standard protocol for companies of all sizes in 2040 to have an active social media division dedicated to customer interaction so that it may shape the social media conversations about the company, its products, and its services.

B. Media

In years past, content created for mass distribution was largely produced by professional television, radio, and film studios.[20] In recent years, however, the majority of newly created content made available online has been produced by amateurs and independent producers.[21] This trend, coupled with advancements in media production software for personal computers, suggests that the overwhelming majority of content producers in 2040 will be the content consumers themselves.

Another factor that will likely spur amateur content creators is the architectural shift in content distribution platforms from broadcasting channels to internet streams.[22] With the broadcast medium, programming had to be transmitted at a specific time and on a specific channel,[23] but the shift to streaming content online renders broadcast time irrelevant and allows a user to time-shift, access, and consume content at her own convenience. As online viewing becomes more widely accepted, the likely result will be that content producers make more of their content available exclusively online.[24] If this is so, then perhaps in 30 years, most professional television programming will only be streamed to consumers online rather than transmitted over traditional broadcast mediums. This personalization would effectively un-bundle the current channel packages offered by cable and satellite companies, and give the user greater control over the specific type of content she wishes to access.

C. Privacy

The proliferation of online social media as a primary means for communication and content creation will also affect how individuals, groups, business, and the government approach privacy issues. Their approaches will be predicated upon the social norms with respect to privacy existing in 2040. Thus, this Part of the essay will explore these possible social norms, Part IV will take up the public policy issues related to privacy, and Part V will explore some potential legal responses to these challenges.

Facebook founder Mark Zuckerberg declared last year that privacy "was no longer a 'social norm'" and argued that social norms have evolved to the point where persons are comfortable with sharing multiple kinds of information "more openly and with more people."[25] While the merits of Zuckerberg's claim may be debated, his rejection of a private internet may reflect an architectural reality that has already been built into the online world.[26] By employing cookies[27] and web beacons[28], all types of organizations would be able to monitor a user's online activities without explicit permission to do so.[29] The problem, in short, is that "surveillance is not self-authenticating" in cyberspace.[30] Given these challenges, the question becomes whether online surveillance *could* become self-authenticating, and if so, whether it will achieve that state 30 years from now.

These questions may be answered by considering the existing trends in online privacy. Although Zuckerberg rejected privacy as a social norm[31], his claim, even if accurate, would not reject user control of privacy as a social norm. The uproar stemming from Facebook's decision to change its Terms of Service (TOS) regarding user-uploaded content[32] suggests there is a deeply-seeded norm where users believe they *ought to be in control* of the information they share, even if they make that information semi-public. Even Zuckerberg acknowledged this reality when, in response to the controversy, he wrote, "Our philosophy is that people own their information and control who they share it with."[33] If this is so, then this trend suggests that it is more likely than not that a robust desire to preserve individual control of privacy will persist through the year 2040.

D. The Legal Industry

Finally, the increased availability of information and the internet's global presence may lead to a number of changes in the legal industry. First, increased abilities to analyze social media content and mine them for relevant data may create new ways for attorneys to identify and target clients. For instance, family law and personal injury attorneys may be able to use social networks to identify users in their areas who have recently shared content that would suggest the users' need for legal representation. Second, the internet's global nature may lead the legal industry down one of two very distinct paths. On one hand, law firms may grow larger through mergers in order to maximize the benefits of economies of scale and vertical integration.[34] On the other hand, the internet's broader reach may help sustain more boutique firms by making it easier for the firm to find clients needing help with specialized legal issues.

IV.   Potential Problems and Public Policy Issues

It is likely that privacy issues will remain the paramount problem in cyber law over the next three decades. Challenges arising from privacy may be divided into two categories: 1) issues involving the government; and 2) issues among private parties. Since the structure of the social media model emphasizes the decentralized interactions between private content producers and consumers, this analysis will focus solely on the latter category.[35]

Privacy issues among private parties typically involve contractual agreements or self-regulatory principles.[36] An exception to this rule arises when private entities either serve a public function or operate as the nexus "between the government and the private party."[37] Typical issues stemming from these non-governmental privacy concerns include: whether a company's TOS is appropriate and optimal; whether and to what extent an individual may be able to maintain some level of online privacy; and whether the internet may become a new type of public forum so that certain Constitutional guarantees would attach.

V.   Some Responses to Emerging Problems

There are several ways to respond to the privacy issues mentioned in Part IV. First, one possible way to develop an optimal TOS is to encourage the appropriate parties in the private sector to develop a set of self-regulatory principles that would help standardize the provisions in a TOS.[38] Drafters of an optimal TOS would need to account for the interests of both the consumers and the online content creators. This will be more likely to occur given the social media model's tendency to collapse these previously distinct groups. Second, one possible way to preserve some semblance of online privacy may be the development of a online "do not track" database that would be akin to the current "do not call" registry for telemarketers.[39] This may conceivably take shape either as a centralized database of IP addresses or a line of code that could be incorporated into devices wishing to opt-out of certain types of online tracking. Finally, as the internet increasingly becomes the primary place for citizens to engage in the marketplace of ideas, courts may come to recognize certain internet spaces as digital public forums that are functionally equivalent to traditional public forums, and thus hold them to the same standard of scrutiny.[40]

VI.   Conclusion

In these ways, the year 2040 may be characterized by a "Big Family" where the members of a decentralized online community of content producers and creators are able to engage one another in dynamic and continuous conversations.

---

[1] NICHOLAS JOHNSON, *Communications and the Year* 2000, *in* HOW TO TALK BACK TO YOUR TELEVISION SET 119 (1970).

[2] *Id.* at 122.

[3] *See generally* Red Lion Broadcasting Co. v. FCC, 207, 208–10 (describing a broadcasting system where a limited number of groups were licensed by the FCC to distribute content via the airwaves).

[4] *See id.*(identifying the three major groups involved in the lawsuit).

[5] *See generally id.* (discussing the relatively scarcity of broadcast channels "where there are substantially more individuals who want to broadcast than there are frequencies to allocate." *Id.*).

[6] *What We Do*, FEDERAL COMMUNICATIONS COMMISSION,
 http://www.fcc.gov/what-we-do (last visited Nov. 17, 2011).

[7] Deb Roy, *The Birth of a word*, TED (Mar. 2011)
http://www.ted.com/talks/deb_roy_the_birth_of_a_word.html.

[8]   Clay   Shirky,   *How   social   media   can   make   history*   (Jun.   2009)

http://www.ted.com/talks/clay_shirky_how_cellphones_twitter_facebook_can_make_ history.html ("The internet is the first medium in history that has native support for groups and conversation at the same time. Whereas the phone gave us the one-to-one pattern, and television, radio, magazines and books gave us the one-to-many pattern, the internet gives us the many-to-many pattern. For the first time, media is natively good at supporting these types of conversations" *Id.*).

[9] Roy, *The Birth of a word.*

[10] Shirky, *How social media can make history*, ("Members of the former audience . . . can now also be producers and not consumers. Every time a new consumer joins this media landscape, a new producer joins as well because the same equipment—phones, computers—lets you consume and produce. It's as if when you bought a book they threw in the printing press for free; it's like you had a phone that could turn into a radio if you pressed the right buttons." *Id.*).

[11] *See, supra* notes 3–6 and accompanying text.

[12] *See* Roy, *The Birth of a word.* (Identifying the different structures of social media-based discussions of content. Structurally, these conversations may take on three different forms. First, the discussion may take the form of a "co-viewing clique" or "virtual living room" where a piece of content or event causes one consumer to talk with others about the content in real time, which in turn drives additional viewership to the content. Second, the discussion may be driven by an individual such as a professional or amateur critic that shares her thoughts on a piece of content and compels her subscribers to seek out that content themselves. Lastly, certain events or types of content may be able to drive the conversations themselves. These would typically include monumental events such as Presidential State of the Union addresses or national tragedies).

[13] Shirky, *How social media can make history.*

[14] Nicholas Johnson, *The Breadth of Cyber and Electronics Impact* http://www.uiowa.edu/~cyberlaw/CEL/CEL11ElectronicsImpact.html (last visited Nov. 20, 2011). Regrettably, limitations upon length prevents this essay from exploring all eight of the categories impacted by developments in cyber and electronic technology. The eight categories are: business, international, legal, life, media, privacy, technology, and other. *Id.*

[15] This proactive quest for feedback may have been accomplished in a number of ways, including focus groups, questionnaires, and surveys. Eric Garner. *Customer Feedback Techniques*, BUSINESSKNOWHOW.COM http://www.businessknowhow.com/marketing/customer-feedback.htm (last visited Nov. 20, 2011).

[16] *Online Social Media Principles*, The Coca-Cola Company (Dec. 15, 2009) http://www.viralblog.com/wp-content/uploads/2010/01/TCCC-Online-Social-Media-Principles-12-2009.pdf/; *Social Media Tips*, Eastman Kodak Company (2010) http://www.kodak.com/US/images/en/corp/aboutKodak/onlineToday/Social_Media _10_7aSP.pdf.

[17] *Online Social Media Principles*, The Coca-Cola Company at 2–3.

[18] *Social Media Tips*, Eastman Kodak Company at 2, 7.

[19] For example, Netflix recently angered its customers when it significantly increased the price of its services and briefly proposed splitting its services into two separate companies, which would have necessitated users wanting both types of services to create an additional account. Cliff Edwards, *Netflix Declines Most Since 2004 After Losing*

800,000   U.S.   Subscribers,   Bloomberg   (Oct.   25,   2011)
http://www.bloomberg.com/news/2011-10-25/netflix-declines-most-since-2004-after-losing-800-000-u-s-subscribers.html.The response, spurred on by outrage expressed on Twitter and other social media sites have resulted in the loss of more than 800,000 subscriptions for Netflix in just one quarter. *Id.* Another example of consumer's ability to influence corporate decisions via social media may be seen in Bank of America's decision to abandon a plan that would charge its customers a $5 monthly fee for using its debit card. Tara Siegel Bernard, *In Retreat, Bank of America Cancels Debit Card Fee,* NY TIMES   (Nov.   1,   2011)   *available*   *at* http://www.nytimes.com/2011/11/02/business/bank-of-america-drops-plan-for-debit-card-fee.html.

[20] Shirky, *How social media can make history.*

[21] *Id.* For instance, much user-generated content is often made available through free hosting sites such as Youtube <http://www.youtube.com/> and DailyMotion <http://www.dailymotion.com/us>.

[22] *Id.*

[23] An exception to this rule may be the "Video On Demand" channels offered by cable and satellite companies in more recent years. *Video On Demand,* WIKIPEDIA http://en.wikipedia.org/wiki/Video_on_demand (last visited Nov. 20, 2011).

[24] For example, online content distribution websites such as Hulu.com have already begun producing and airing original content exclusively available online. Brenna Ehrlich, *Hulu Makes First Full-Length Show: Morgan Spurlock's A Day in The Life,* MASHABLE.COM (Aug. 30, 2011) http://mashable.com/2011/08/03/hulu-spurlock/.

[25] Bobbie Johnson, *Privacy No Longer A Social Norm, Says Facebook Founder,* THE GUARDIAN (Jan. 10, 2010)
 http://www.guardian.co.uk/technology/2010/jan/11/facebook-privacy.

[26] Mya Frazier, *On Facebook and Online, Privacy is Only an Illusion,* MEDIASHIFT (Feb. 11, 2011)   http://www.pbs.org/mediashift/2011/02/on-facebook-and-online-privacy-is-only-an-illusion042.html.
"Almost all privacy mechanisms available to users today are based on access control: users can specify which other users are able to view the content or information they upload," the researchers wrote. "Our results show, however, that even information that is not provided by users can sometimes be inferred from the user's location in the network." In other words, our online networks reflect commonalities easily inferred by even the most basic of algorithms. Just by joining -- often under the illusion of privacy -- we reveal ourselves. *Id.*

[27] *HTTP Cookie,* WIKIPEDIA http://en.wikipedia.org/wiki/HTTP_cookie (last visited Nov. 21, 2011).

[28] *Web Bug,* WIKIPEDIA http://en.wikipedia.org/wiki/Web_beacons (last visited Nov. 21, 2011).

[29] Frazier, *On Facebook and Online.*

[30] Lawrence Lessig, *The Law of the Horse: What Cyberlaw Might Teach* 6, 7–8.

[31] Frazier, *On Facebook and Online.*

[32] *Note on the Facebook Controversy,* 200, 201. Facebook amended its Terms of Service by omitting the words "automatically expire" from the following licensing clause: "You may remove your User Content from the Site at any time. If you choose to remove your User Content, the license granted above will automatically expire, however you

acknowledge that the Company may retain archived copies of your User Content." *Id.* in doing so, the "Facebook license extends to adopt users' content perpetually and irrevocably years after the content has been deleted." *Id.*

[33] *Id.*

[34] For example, although the current trend is for law firms out outsource the more mundane aspects of legal work to third-party companies, there is no reason that law firms may not eventually acquire these processing companies and bring them "in-house." This strategy would allow the firm to retain the relatively low cost of outsourced legal work while increasing its profit margins by cutting out the middle man. *See* Elie Mystal, *Thompson Reuters Exploring Sale of BAR/BRI, Will Acquire Pangea3*, ABOVETHELAW (Nov. 18, 2010) http://abovethelaw.com/2010/11/thomson-reuters-exploring-sale-of-barbri-acquire-pangea3/ (Reporting Thompson Reuters's acquisition of an India-based legal outsourcing company).

[35] Once again, limitations upon length have necessitated an incomplete treatment of this issue. For a more complete exploration of this subject, see *Katz*, 309; *Kyllo*, 313; and *Warshak*, 320.

[36] *See generally* Chapter Four, Section A, "Private Regulation" 168–202.

[37] *Applying Constitutional Norms to "Private" Entities*, 203, 203–04. For example, a privately-owned company town is nevertheless "treated as though it were publically held [since] . . . in all other respects [the town] had the characteristics of any other American town." *Marsh v. Alabama*, 204.

[38] A similar approach is already being taken for Online Behavioral Advertising. American Assoc. of Advertising Agencies et. al, *Self-Regulatory Principles for Online Behavioral Advertising* (Jul. 2009), *available at* http://www.iab.net/media/file/ven-principles-07-01-09.pdf.

[39] *Homepage*, NAT'L DO NOT CALL REGISTRY, https://www.donotcall.gov/ (last visited Nov 21, 2011).

[40] *See* Brown v. Louisiana, 383 U.S. 131 (1966) (recognizing libraries as non-traditional public forums).

Chapter 4

How Achievements in Communication Will Alter the Law
Net Neutrality, Online Search Engines, and the Fourth Amendment in the Year 2040

Susan P. Elgin

Communication in the year 2040 will be faster, more accessible, and omnipresent. People will have instantaneous access to others around the world at the push of a button. Everyone—from very young children to the elderly—will carry smartphone-like devices, paper will be a relic of the past, and nearly all items will have computer chips embedded in them. Shoes will be able to tell you how far you've run, thermostats will adjust automatically to your living habits, and shower heads will tell you how much water you've used. The concept of "long distance" will disappear and the world will function more as one community, rather than separate geographic regions.[1]

At the same time, the quality of news reporting will decrease. Consumers will continue to demand free access to content, which will cause newspapers to suffer financially. Many quality, reliable sources of information will fold, unable to compete with cheap sources of information such as blogs. The rise of news outlets funded by corporations and political parties will dominate, and the amount of misinformation will exceed well-reported journalism. The year 2040 will lack quality information and reporting, and therefore maintaining a free and accessible Internet, absent of censorship or manipulation, should hopefully remain a public priority for the continuation of a strong democracy.

I. Net Neutrality and Regulation of the Internet in the Year 2040

Currently, in the year 2011, there is a debate over net neutrality and how to regulate the Internet.[2] By 2040, this will be resolved in favor of declining to try to regulate the Internet.[3] The logistical barriers[4] to regulation are too numerous to overcome,[5] and since the benefits of regulation are dubious,[6] while the concerns regarding regulation are plentiful,[7] purposefully choosing not to regulate the Internet is the responsible choice, and one the public is most likely to demand.[8] While not regulated by law, Internet regulations will remain regulated as they are now: through social norms, markets, architecture, and traditional legal causes of action.[9]

In fact, the ubiquity and reliance on networked technology will be so heightened that Internet access will be considered a right—rather than just another medium[10] of communication or simply a privilege—by 2040. People depend on the availability of this networked world daily for business transactions, commerce, and even interpersonal relationships. Prior to 2040, the government will need to respond to the public will by maintaining net neutrality. The government should also make sure everyone has the Internet available at a reasonable price, or for those without a computer or the ability to pay a reasonable price for Internet access, make it available for free at a public library.[11]

II.   The Role of Search Engines in the Year 2040

In the future, Internet search engines will have even more importance in daily life. Currently, many people search Google regularly, if not many times a day, in search of accurate information. As people become more and more reliant on Google searches as a source (if not the only source) of obtaining information, Google or another similar search engine will become exponentially more powerful.[12] Currently, Google uses a page ranking algorithm that is viewpoint neutral and based on the relevance to the search and the overall importance of the website.[13]

By 2040, reliance on this seemingly "viewpoint-neutral" algorithm will be exceptionally important, since the pages near the top are most likely be the websites users read.[14] Because of this, the public has an interest in maintaining the neutrality of the page rank algorithm so the information disseminated is not manipulated by outside parties or the government. This free and unencumbered access to information is vital to maintaining a strong democracy, which is why the Supreme Court is likely to overrule the case *Search King, Inc. v. Google Technology, Inc.* by 2040.[15] The case determined that PageRanks are opinions that are protected by the First Amendment, which could have potentially disastrous consequences for the public. If Google executives are able to control what pages are ranked highly when searched, Google could become politicized and any ideas or viewpoints the company disagrees with could be ranked far below pages that have ideas the company agrees with. This will greatly impede the free flow of information, and the courts are likely to find that PageRanks should remain strictly a mathematical formula devoid of opinion and therefore not deserving of First Amendment protections.[16]

There are several ways this will be dealt with by the year 2040. As discussed earlier in the paper, the net neutrality debate is likely to disappear, with the Internet maintaining its chaotic, end-to-end format without oversight from a regulating body.[17] Therefore, it is unlikely that Google will be regulated in any fashion, unless Google would appoint a self-governing board[18] or willingly cede some regulatory control to the FCC,[19] who would help solve these issues and help maintain Google's position as a trusted source that is free from censorship or manipulation.[20]

Frank Pasquale offers another solution to this problem in his essay *Rankings, Reductionism, and Responsibility*.[21] If Google was upset with search results (for example, if the search for "Jew" produced a Holocaust-denial website as a top hit),[22] the company could add an asterisk to the PageRank, explaining why the page appears.[23] In addition, individuals who may have something unflattering, or even incorrect, about them on the Internet, could also edit these asterisks. This provides a person with the opportunity to "give one's own side of the story."[24] By the year 2040, information will be even more accessible, instantaneous, and unforgiving. Small blips on a record will remain forever enshrined on the Internet, and while the next section will discuss how privacy expectations will have evolved by 2040, providing the opportunity for as much information as possible through the self-regulation of search engines is in the public interest in this case.

III.   Privacy in the Year 2040: The Fourth Amendment

In the year 2040, the legal standard of privacy for Fourth Amendment purposes will still be the *Katz* test: "[W]hether the individual has an expectation of privacy that society is prepared to recognize as reasonable."[25] While this will remain the standard, the application of this in 2040 will be completely unrecognizable by today's standards. If the Supreme Court continues to use *Kyllo*'s enunciation of privacy including an evaluation of whether the device involved was in common use,[26] then this reasonable expectation of privacy standard could become whittled away to the point where it is rendered nearly meaningless by the year 2040.

For example, the Supreme Court recently encountered a Fourth Amendment claim in the case *United States v. Jones*, which has yet to be decided by the Court.[27] The District Court said that the use of a GPS to monitor a suspect's whereabouts amounted to an "Orwellian intrusion" and said the court has to "begin to address whether revolutionary changes in technology require changes to existing Fourth Amendment doctrine."[28] The outcome of this case will likely hint at the future of the Fourth Amendment: The Court could decide this breach of privacy was not reasonable, or the Court could just as easily decide that GPS devices are now in regular public use, and that outside of the home, the suspect had no expectation of privacy.

No matter how the Court rules in *Jones*, privacy will most certainly be eroded to the point of an unblinking eye by the year 2040. For example, by the year 2040, there may be technology that includes devices such as a car that drives itself by plugging in a destination address. In that situation, GPS devices will be in common use, so a person would likely not maintain a reasonable expectation of privacy in the addresses entered into the device. In the *Jones* case, the Court of Appeals said this type of information could reveal information such as "whether [the person] is a weekly churchgoer, a heavy drinker, a regular at the gym, an unfaithful husband, an outpatient receiving medical treatment, an associate of particular individuals or political groups — and not just one such fact about a person, but all such facts."[29]

But is this a problem? Will the public actually object to having his or her actions recorded, or will it make everyone more secure?[30] As long as you have nothing to hide, and no reason to be under surveillance, would most oppose having law enforcement know this kind of information, especially if it can be used to deter crime?[31] By the year 2040, privacy outside of the home will be non-existent, as surveillance cameras will be commonplace in shops to catch shoplifters, stoplights to catch red light runners, and highways to catch speeders.[32] Even if the Court in *Jones* says the police needed a warrant for GPS surveillance, this type of information will only become more detailed, available, and commonplace in the future.

IV.   Privacy in the Year 2040: Online Privacy

In addition to physical privacy, people will also have online personas that will also create privacy issues. Obviously, that person has put some personal information online purposefully, on websites such as Facebook and LinkedIn.[33] This creates a paradox of sorts, which Facebook founder Mark Zuckerberg addressed after Facebook changed its privacy settings, which upset many users.[34] By the year 2040, this purposeful sharing of information will become a bright line: Those who wish to share information can, and those who do not want to share will be able to maintain their privacy. However, once that information is online, the user loses any expectation of privacy, even if that person reasonably believes in the security of Facebook privacy controls,[35] since by the year 2040, those controls will most likely be superficial and easily susceptible to hacking and overrides.[36]

While information a person chooses to share online—even if that person thinks the information may be able to stay private—an additional concern online will be information about a person that the person *did not* choose to share. For example, the Iowa Supreme Court recently ruled that criminal records could remain online without a violation of due process or equal protection rights.[37] By 2040, there will only be electronic records, because as discussed above, everyone will have some types of smartphone device and paper will mostly be a relic of the past. Most courts will likely follow the Iowa court's determination to allow these records to remain online. As discussed earlier, Google could allow an asterisk next to the search so the person could tell his or her side of the story, although this will probably be deemed unnecessary.[38] In 2040, small indiscretions will stay with an individual forever, as the Internet is an unforgiving source of information with a never-ending memory.

V.   How the Practice of Law Will Change by 2040

How criminal charges and other public records are accessed (and how to get those removed) will be one area of the law that lawyers will need to know in the year 2040. The quickened pace of the world will also impact law, and although the law will continue to change and evolve, it will lag behind the lightning pace of technological development. In addition, lawyers will be expected to be available on-call.[39] Most legal services will be available over the Internet, both through online forms or live consultations with available lawyers. In addition, increased communication through video conferencing and the Internet will create more specialized law firms that will represent clients all over the world. The increased likelihood of a global community will create more standardized laws throughout jurisdictions and online, traditional causes of action, such as libel or other torts, will be the only way to control content. Since law is likely to lag behind technology, lawyers will need to be creative in adapting existing forms of law to new methods of communication and surveillance to achieve the best outcomes for their clients.

---

[1] In David R. Johnson and David G. Post's essay *Law and Borders—The Rise of Law in Cyberspace*, the authors discuss the role of geographic boundaries in attempting to regulate the Internet.

[2] To see the FCC's *Proposed Rules: Preserving the Open Internet, Broadband Industry Practices*, including the six rules for broadband Internet providers, see textbook pages 254-257.

[3] While no regulation will be the default, traditional causes of action, such as torts, libel, fraud, etc. occurring on the Internet could still be subject to legal action. By using the phrase "no regulation," this paper means no government or corporation will own the Internet, and it will remain free from censorship and accessible to all with a computer.

[4] In David G. Post's essay *Against Cyberanarchy* (textbook pages 92-97), Post discusses how human activity was geographically constrained in the 1950s. Now with the Internet, a global network that has the ability to connect everyone, and people are "(virtually) equidistant from one another, irrespective of their location in real space." Textbook page 96. In the 1950s, there was less legal border-crossing and jurisdiction confusion, and the only examples Post cites of this were "airplane crashes, mass torts, and multinational commercial transactions." Textbook page 97.

[5] In Jack L. Goldsmith's essay *The Internet and the Abiding Significance of Territorial Sovereignty* (textbook pages 84-89) the author cites the three arguments against regulation of the Internet:

> First, territorial regulation of the Internet is not feasible because the source of Internet transactions can easily be located outside of the regulating sovereign's territory. Second, unilateral territorial regulation of the Internet leads to overlapping and often inconsistent regulation of the same transaction. Third, unilateral regulation of the Internet produces significant, normatively problematic spillover effects.

Textbook page 85. While Goldsmith ultimately rejects these, the concerns are legitimate and unable to be fully overcome. Goldsmith discusses "offshore regulation evasion" by other countries (textbook page 87), but concludes that even if the regulations are mostly futile, it "need not be perfect to be effective" to some extent. Textbook page 88.

[6] In the case *La Ligue Contre le Racisme el l'Antisémitisme v. Yahoo!, Inc.*, a French court finds that the United States website Yahoo! violated French law by allowing Nazi items to be auctioned on its website. Textbook pages 99-101. The French court sanctions Yahoo! for violating French law, but ultimately, the French court could do nothing to enforce the judgment. In the textbook notes following the case, the textbook authors hypothesize the potential effect of foreign jurisdictions attempting to enforce their laws on websites owned in different countries. One possible outcome would be for website owners to try to conform to laws worldwide, which could result in an Internet representative of the "*most restrictive* community." Textbook page 102.

[7] In David G. Post's essay *Of Black Holes and Decentralized Law-Making in Cyberspace* (textbook pages 178-181), Post discusses the policy choices for regulating the Internet, including "order versus chaos," and ultimately determines that chaos is preferable because it encourages growth and innovation. Textbook page 181. Post writes:

> A 'stable' Internet is one locked in place, incapable of generating

innovative responses to the very problems that it is itself bringing into existence . . . there are some problems that are best solved by these messy, disordered, semi-chaotic, unplanned, decentralized systems, and that the costs that necessarily accompany such unplanned disorder may sometimes be worth bearing.

[8] See Editorial, "Taking Aim at Internet Rules" from the *New York Times*, Nov. 9, 2011, page A34 (a discussion about how the Senate's expected vote on stripping the FCC of authority to enforce rules that prohibit Internet service providers from censoring or burying "transmission of content that might compete with their own."). See the website http://www.savetheinternet.com/ for an overview of the proponents for net neutrality.

[9] Lawrence Lessig, *The Law of the Horse: What Cyberlaw Might Teach*, textbook pages 9-10.

[10] In Jack L. Goldsmith's essay *The Internet and the Abiding Significance of Territorial Sovereignty*, textbook ages 84-89, Goldsmith tries to assert that the Internet is simply another medium comparable to the telephone or telegraph. Textbook page 85. However, the global design of the Internet and the capabilities of the Internet—which includes financial and commercial transactions, as well as a mode of communication—create additional implications, which means that "effective regulation will require national, and more likely global, cooperation." Quote from *American Libraries Association v. Pataki*, textbook page 109.

[11] In *Mainstream Loudoun v. Board of Trustees of the Loudoun County Public Library*, the court said the library could not create content-based restrictions for patrons accessing the Internet at the library, as any sort of censorship was contrary to the First Amendment as a content-based restriction.

[12] The government could subject Google to regulation under antitrust laws, if Google does prevail as the only reliable and preferred search engine in existence by the year 2040. However, this paper will not discuss this possibility, and will instead focus on First Amendment concerns implicated by Google's power to select the information that appears from searches in the form of PageRanks.

[13] Frank Pasquale, *Rankings, Reductionism, and Responsibility*, Textbook page 233.

[14] For an explanation of how Google operates the PageRank algorithm, see *Search King, Inc. v. Google Technology, Inc.* on Textbook page 230. This numerical representation is derived from factors such as text-matching and also by counting the number of other websites that link to the website. While these are neutral factors, they are not fool proof and are capable of being manipulated by both Google and outside companies.

[15] *Search King, Inc. v. Google Technology, Inc.*, Textbook pages 230-232. In the case, the court considers whether Google PageRanks have First Amendment protection. The court says yes, determining that the PageRanks are opinions. While the algorithm is "objective in nature," since Google has the ability to manipulate the results to the company's liking (such as burying websites they do not want to be highly ranked, such as competitors or companies that sell services which would help others manipulate the PageRank algorithm) and because the algorithm itself is designed to place the most significant websites at the top, the court says that the process of ranking pages is "fundamentally subjective in nature." Due to this subjectivity, the court concludes that PageRanks are opinions deserving of First Amendment protections, which shields Google from tort liability, which in this case arose out of Google's "intentional manipulation" of the PageRanks.

[16] The court says that "PageRanks relate to matters of public concern," which is why

they are deserving of First Amendment protection. Textbook page 232. This part of the court's reasoning is sound, and it is valid that the court would have an interest in shielding Google and other search engines from potential tort liability due to the content and result of the searches. However, the conclusion that PageRanks—which should be a neutral, numerical outcome based on an algorithm—are opinions with First Amendment protection is dubious at best. This conclusion gives Google free reign to do whatever the company wants with the searches, allowing Google itself, although essentially foreclosing any outsiders' ability to do so, to manipulate the PageRanks. Giving this much discretion to Google to do whatever the company would like is not in the public's interest, and if the court truly believes that PageRanks are "of public concern," which they state in the opinion, then the court's holding is a non sequitur and likely to be re-examined and refined before the year 2040 to keep the conclusion more consistent with the public interest.

[17] For an explanation of how the Internet's end-to-end design allows for the Internet's vast "growth and utilization" by allowing user autonomy and freedom, see textbook page 23.

[18] This board could be composed of everyone from communication experts and policymakers to just regular, everyday users of Google. For controversies (such as how to handle an outside company that is attempting to act as a middleman to manipulate PageRanks, like was the case in *Search King, Inc.*) the Google Board could solicit input from the public, debate the issue amongst the board, and issue an opinion summarizing and explaining what action Google was going to take and why. This type of transparency will help the public trust and participate in these types of controversies without intervention from the courts or regulation by the government.

[19] This paper emphasizes "willingly" for Google's cessation of total control because the Internet should not, and likely will not, be forced to regulation by the government. The FCC could play a small role, and Google could bring in the FCC as a neutral, experienced oversight expert for issues such as the *Search King* case. The public values an Internet that is free from government and corporation restraint, and as Philip J. Weiser writes in *Internet, Governance, Standard Setting, and Self-Regulation*, it is due to these "open standards that has allowed the Internet to grow exponentially as a network of networks" and that the public values the premise that "the Internet meant that no one owned the Internet's protocols or had to pay a license for their use." Textbook page 169.

[20] Another option would be for the FTC to play a supervisory role, as PageRanks could arguably affect consumers. The FTC has intervened in Google operations before, when the commission made Google clearly distinguish between PageRanks that were a genuine result of the algorithm, and those websites that had paid for a top-ranking slot. The FTC did this to "advance fair competition in the search market ... to put in place basic procedural protections for those potentially harmed by query results." Textbook page 237.

[21] Textbook pages 232-238.

[22] Example comes from textbook page 234. In response to this real situation, Google added a headline to the website which read "An explanation of our search results," and if the user clicked on it, Google would explain the algorithm method and why this website appeared. Explaining how the algorithm works helps "distance" Google from the results of their searches.

[23] Textbook page 237. Pasquale asserts that this could be done "at minimal cost" to

Google and would help correct any information that might be false or misleading.

[24] Textbook page 237. Pasquale recommends allowing this for individuals after the company (or perhaps a different governing body, such as an oversight board of some sort, or the FTC) finds a complaint "meritorious."

[25] Quote from *Kyllo v. United States*, textbook page 315. *Kyllo* also explains that, while "reasonable" may be an unclear and subjective standard, the court can look at factors such as the person's belief of privacy or whether or not the technology used to collect information is in common public use.

[26] In *Kyllo*, the Supreme Court concluded that the thermal imaging device used—which was aimed at the house from the street to record heightened temperatures indicative of growing illegal marijuana plants—was not in common public use, and therefore, the defendant in *Kyllo* maintained a reasonable expectation of privacy because he could not anticipate that a device such as this would be used to obtain information about what he did within his home.

[27] In *Jones*, the Court will decide if police need a warrant to attach a GPS device to a suspect's car in order to track his movements for extended periods of time. *See* Adam Liptak, "Court Case Asks if 'Big Brother' Is Spelled GPS" from the *New York Times*, Sept. 10, 2011, page A1.

[28] Quote from Judge Nicholas G. Garaufis of the Federal District Court in Brooklyn, from Adam Liptak, "Court Case Asks if 'Big Brother' Is Spelled GPS" from the *New York Times*, Sept. 10, 2011, page A1.

[29] Quote from Judge Douglas H. Ginsburg of the United States Court of Appeals for the District of Columbia Circuit, from Adam Liptak, "Court Case Asks if 'Big Brother' Is Spelled GPS" from the *New York Times*, Sept. 10, 2011, page A1.

[30] In Daniel J. Solove's essay *Conceptualizing Privacy* (textbook pages 627-634), Solove argues that privacy is evolving and that people have come to expect less privacy. On page 634, he suggests that the government is able to "gradually condition people to accept wiretapping or other privacy incursions, thus altering society's expectations of privacy." However, he does suggest that privacy expectations will happen to "adapt to the changing realities of the modern world."

[31] In Jonathan Zittrain's essay *The Future of the Internet—and How to Stop It* (textbook pages 700-705) he uses an example from Texas in 2006. The state set up cameras along the Mexico border and placed the video feed on the Internet. Textbook page 703. The public tuned in to this live video and the state encouraged people to report suspicious activity. In just one month, the state had received 13,000 emails that lead to seizing four hundred pounds of marijuana, recovering a stolen car, and stopping a dozen undocumented immigrants.

[32] In Jonathan Zittrain's essay *The Future of the Internet—and How to Stop It* (textbook page 704) he explains what he calls "Privacy 2.0." He argues that surveillance will not simply be limited to law enforcement, but also peer-to-peer technologies and shopping malls. He attributes this to shifts in technology, including cheap processors, cheap networks, cheap sensors, and cheap surveillance cameras. Textbook pages 701-702. Zittrain suggests that in the future, whenever a person is in public, that person is "on notice" that his or her actions could be captured by a mobile phone video and easily uploaded to the Internet in a matter of seconds. Textbook page 704.

[33] While adults are free to share as much information as they like on these social networking sites, the FTC currently regulates websites that collect information from

children without permission from their parents. See Somini Sengupta, "Regulators Say Social Network Violated Child Privacy Law," *The New York Times*, Nov. 8, 2011. By 2040, the ubiquity of the Internet will likely change this, and rather than banning children under 13 from social networking, children will grow up with online profiles and will be active participants online at a very young age.

[34] In the *Note on the Facebook Controversy*, Zuckerberg "explained the paradox created when people want to share their information (phone number, pictures, email address, etc.) with the public, but at the same time desire to remain in complete control of who has access to this info." Textbook page 201.

[35] For example, people who write nasty things about their bosses online should not expect that information to remain private, nor should people who upload unflattering, unprofessional pictures. Much of these privacy concerns can be solved by simply using common sense and only sharing information a person would be comfortable letting the world know.

[36] Facebook maintains "Facebook Principles," as well as a "Statement of Rights and Responsibilities" for users to learn about the site's privacy controls. However, those have been changed constantly since the beginning of the site, and Zuckerberg has said he expects users to "familiarize themselves with the products" before using them, since "Facebook is still in the business of introducing new and therefore potentially disruptive technology." Textbook page 201.

[37] *Judicial Branch & State Court Administrator v. Iowa District Court for Linn County*, No. 10-0163 (Iowa July 15, 2011) *available at*
http://www.iowacourtsonline.org/Supreme_Court/Recent_Opinions/20110715/10-0163.pdf. A man was charged with public intoxication and while the charge was later dismissed, the charge remained on his record, including the easily accessible Iowa Court Online database. While the man did not demand removal from the hard copy of his record, he did want the charge removed from computer databases, which are easily accessed by anyone running a Google search of his name. In addition, the man claimed an equal protection violation, since defendants who receive deferred judgments were able to expunge the charge from the online record, while those whose charges were dismissed or found not guilty were unable to do so. The court recognized the role in the Internet plays in privacy issues, but declined to require the removal of criminal charges from the online court database, saying:

> This case illustrates the impact of the internet on our daily affairs. Dockets always have been public records, but until the Iowa state court dockets became computerized and available on-line, it was not easy for the public to use them. Now, one can learn of any person's past involvement with Iowa's court system by making a few mouse clicks and a few strokes at a keyboard.

The court resolved the case mainly on legislative purpose and statutory interpretation principles, and noted that the decision did not foreclose the possibility that these types of charges (those that result in a dismissal or acquittal) may be removed in the future, if the legislature or court administrators thought it necessary.

[38] Frank Pasquale, *Rankings, Reductionism, and Responsibility*, Textbook page 237. In Pasquale's essay, he suggests adding the asterisk for "false or misleading" search results, which is unlikely to include real criminal charges. Instead, Pasquale recommends this

type of remedy for situations such as a search of a man's name that comes up with a website "Don't Date Him, Girl," which has malicious information about men posted by ex-girlfriends. Textbook page 234.

[39] From Cyber and Electronic Impact, John Schwartz, "Delivering a Lawyer Within 15 Minutes (Soda Extra)," *The New York Times*, June 17, 2011, A21.

Chapter 5

Analogizing Our Way to 2040
Tom Evans

I.   General Technology and Communication Innovation

Capacity expands in everything. Computer power will continue to grow. Network speeds and downloads will be magnitudes faster. There will be more security cameras, more robots, more space travel and more gadgets.

The major change in computing will be the migration of processing power and data storage to remote centers. Users will access resources at the remote centers via "network portals". Users will benefit from the synchronization of data and computing. Instead of having a Personal Computer, a netbook, and a cell phone, a user will have one virtual computer which can be accessed by multiple devices. Overall users will have more efficient access because everything will be in one location, accessible from multiple devices or "network portals." Unfortunately, Big Brother will use the advances to further peer into citizens' lives.

Another change will be what communicates. Many more devices will be connected to the global network. Appliances, automobiles, clothing, robots and many other "things" will connect to the global network. Your fridge will be able to automatically generate a grocery list of your food needs by tracking RFID tags on products. The grocery list will then be automatically generated and sent to your virtual computer. Then you access the list from your mobile phone.

Advances in technology will continue to diminish our privacy under the flag of safety and it will threaten our constitutional rights. The Government will be more aware of and better track citizens' movements, actions, and ideas. We will lose much of our autonomy. The question is, will anyone care? Or will a generation raised on Facebook accept Big Brother's presence in their everyday life?

II.   Global Open Peer to Peer Network

A global open peer to peer network will emerge as a response to government regulation of traditional networks. It will start as a patch work in densely populated areas with slow speeds, but eventually evolve to global coverage with function identically to traditional networks. Information packets will travel coast to coast by being passed off from one device to the next in a continuous change until it reaches the destination. Information packets will take multiple paths and be assembled at the final destination much like the current internet. Large scale closed peer to peer networks, called "Darknets," already exist.

The network will harness consumer wireless devices, not corporate built infrastructure. Imagine the Wi-Fi chip in everyone's cell phone and home router being used to create a global web of connections. Information is passed from one individual to the next in a continuous chain until information reaches the destination. The catalyst necessary is an innovator to release free software that is secure and non-technical. Similar to how Napster was the catalyst for peer to peer file sharing that transformed data sharing, software will be the catalyst that transforms peer to peer networking into a viable large scale network.

This network will present problems for governments. The networks will emerge to circumvent government control of traditional networks. Thus the networks will be used by individuals for activities that the government prefers did not happen. Individuals will access these networks to do many things from viewing censored material to downloading copyrighted music. Individuals will have some security concerns, but will benefit from the networks in general.

The protocols and standards will be set by the individual or body that creates the software that connects peers into a network. However this entity will not derive any profit controlling the west coast code because the software will have to be free to encourage mass adoption. Governments will respond legally to the network, but attempts to regulate it won't work. Individuals will ignore government regulation to access unregulated content similarly to how individuals currently ignore laws and download copyrighted material.

III.   Biological Engineering

Scientist will be able to engineer and edit life in the laboratory. The potential applications of biological engineering are limitless. It can be used to create new synthetic life. It can be applied to agriculture for higher yielding livestock and crops. It can be applied to medicine to develop revolutionary treatments. It can be applied to humans to edit our DNA blueprints. It can be used by terrorists to create a global pandemic. For better or worse, the way we think about living organisms will change.

Biological Engineering will raise many moral and political issues. The potential to edit our DNA is great power. We will possess the ability to redesign ourselves into better versions, but how will we use them? To evolve ourselves and correct errors left over from evolution? Will people modify their children to give them an advantage in life? How will our sports leagues be affected when people can enhance strength with Biological Engineering? How will academics competition be affected if intelligence can be engineered? Will "designer DNA" become the norm? If a foreign country engineers a super human and starts filling their society with it, will we be forced to do the same? How do we deal with a virus engineered into a weapon?

Biological Engineering will require government intervention to set limits. There will need to be limits for safety and ethical reasons. Safety limits to protect people who seek new and evolving treatment methods. Ethical limits so we can protect what it means to be humans. The limits may evolve to become more liberal as society becomes more accustom to and comfortable with engineering our species.

Standard setting and oversight should involve the global community like nuclear material. With the potential to engineer a super virus, a rogue state could unleash a global pandemic. Powerful states will be forced to engage rogue states in effective diplomacy to avoid Biological Engineered Warfare because unlike nuclear material, biological material does not emit easily detected radiation.

IV.   Space Travel

Close to earth space travel will be cheaper and more accessible to private citizens. Purposes will be varied. Some travelers will be space tourists going for the experience. Some travelers will be those seeking to travel globally at rates faster than supersonic jets. Corporate and education entities will also have an increased presence in space consistent with their missions. New corporations will emerge to meet the needs of this growing industry.

Nations will continue to explore further out into the space frontier. A permanent base will be built on the Moon or Mars. As the first permanent home off of Earth, the experiment will pave the way for colonizing space. Imagine Jamestown on the Moon or Mars.

Space travel will face hurdles as it becomes more common in society. There will be safety issues and loss of human life. It is endemic of pushing the frontier of transportation. The Hindenburg, the Titanic, and Space Shuttle Challenger were all pushing the frontier of transportation when innocent lives were lost. Fortunately we were able to learn many lessons from the brave adventurers that lost their lives. Those lessons made transportation safer for everyone else. Unfortunately we are going to have to learn some more hard lessons on the way to safe space travel.

Space travel will need to be regulated like other forms of transportation. Rather than create an entirely new agency, it will be more efficient for the FAA to regulate space travel. This will minimize duplication and ensure information sharing between relevant parties. Space jet and airplane traffic will need to be managed to prevent collisions. Space jets could utilize the same airports as jet airplanes. Standards and Regulations to ensure safe space travel would be similar to those already in place to regulate air travel.

Territorial disputes to space real property will become an issue as nations establish permanent space outposts. These disputes will be among the elite powerful nations that seek a strategic advantage from a permanent space presence. Powerful nations will be the only nations capable of managing the logistics necessary to sustain a space base. A sustained presence will be essential to asserting legitimate territorial claims of space real estate.

V.   Climate Engineering

In the battle to combat climate change, technologies to engineer or control climate will emerge. Droughts and storms will be fought with technology. Droughts and storms will be created as weapons. Climate will evolve from a force of nature to a force regulated by the global community.

Climate control may become one of the most important foreign policy issues. Manipulation of climate by one nation could affect every other country in the world. Nations from cold regions would be more welcoming to global warming, compared to those closer to the equator. Agriculture and food production could be hugely impacted by climate manipulation. Additionally accidental climate change will occur on the way to learning how to control the weather.

Climate peace will require global cooperation. Climate changes in one place have global consequences, so this will be the only effective way to address climate issues. Imagine diplomats meeting at global summits to negotiate global climate policy. Powerful nations that can actually manipulate climate will dictate these negotiations. There is also for the potential for disputes domestically, that is between different regions of one nation. In the United States climate engineering will be handled at the Federal level to avoid domestic turmoil.

VI.   Robotics

Robots will perform an increasing number of functions in our society. Robots will mow our yard and clean our house instead of just vacuuming. Robots will conduct police work instead of just warfare. Most importantly, advances in artificial intelligence will allow robots to perform tasks they never learned instead of only tasks they were programmed to perform.

Robots will raise issues as they become more prevalent in society. Is a soldier controlling a robot that accidentally kills a civilian responsible for the death? Who is responsible for an artificially intelligent robot that accidentally causes harm, the manufacturer or the operator? Will we allow robots to police our streets? What limits are we going to place on tasks that can be handled by robots?

Robots and their role in society will need to be regulated at the State and Federal level. Limits will need to be set on robot tasks so that their assignments are safe. Accidents will happen though. Victims of robot caused harm will be able to file court actions for indemnification similar to product liability. Imagine George Jetson taking Rosey's Manufacturor to court for product liability if Rosey harmed Astro.

Chapter 6

Cyber Law and its Ever Changing Landscape
Michael Fleming

The legal landscape of cyber law is changing at a torrid pace. New technological innovations have become commonplace in our lives every year. We have access to the internet from anywhere outside of the most remote places. In thirty years, the technological advances could be staggering. It is very difficult to make specific bold predictions and not look foolish later, so it makes sense to me to speak of more general trends as opposed to any precise inventions that may arise.

One potential battle ground in the next few decades will be the regulation of the internet. The key issue of regulation is if there should be public regulation or private regulation. We will have to make more decisions about whether or not we want the government to intervene in the online arena. There are already battles about this issue now. Although the courts will probably not decide this issue, the prevailing regulatory body will adopt the laws or standards that the courts are to follow. If companies or standard setting bodies make the rules, then there will probably be a more open space with a free flowing exchange of communications and information. However, if the government was allowed to regulate and set rules, I would expect this would close off portions of the internet. I believe the open standards that have built the internet are the best way to proceed and will prevail. However, the government will probably try to legislate more and will no doubt have a greater impact on the internet in the future. My belief is that the internet will remain open with the open protocols being the major regulatory scheme for the internet.

A second issue to consider in the future is free speech on the internet. With the rise of Twitter and Facebook, broadcasting speech on the internet has become easier than ever. It seems very likely to me that more channels will open in the future. I cannot say for certain that there will be many more sites to rival Facebook, but I can say that existing and future sites will establish different ways to operate. Video chatting will probably increase, and other ways to communicate will also open up. It seems extremely likely to me that speech will be able to reach more ears in different ways in the next thirty years. The problems this will create could be significant. The key issue with free speech on the internet would be shielding children from obscene and indecent content. If speech becomes more open, there will be complaints from parents and concerned citizens about the quality of speech on the internet. This could present a problem for constitutional law. Basically, what will the courts protect? I believe the courts will follow a similar model to what they employ now. Fight inducing, obscene or indecent speech will not be allowed. However, the ability to use Twitter to spread fake news causing panic will most likely only increase, and this speech will most likely not be protected in my opinion.

What constitutes property is bound to become more of an issue as well. There will most likely be more open source projects available for free over the internet. There will also be an increase in the number of websites and internet users since more people around the globe will gain access to computers. This will create an even bigger network of people and more "property" on the internet. So, the key question with this issue will be what constitutes property on the internet. Will open source books be considered property? Will websites? Do site administrators have property rights in their online material if they make it available for everyone to see? Although I do believe that website creators will have access to change and own their information on the web, it could present contentious issues in intellectual property law. Copyright problems should only increase, and the courts may increase the scope of the fair use doctrine by allowing more access to copyrighted works.

There will be more technologies used to spy on citizens. There will also be more technologies used to make searches. GPS will become more and more ordinary. GPS seems to be the tool most widely used today by the public, and its prevalence should only increase in the next few decades. The government will most likely be allowed more latitude from the courts in using this technology. Once it becomes a widely used technology by the general public, the government will be able to use it more often and in more ways than it does currently. The use of cameras will also increase. Cameras are ubiquitous in our lives now, and it is nearly impossible to walk a block in a city and not get caught on film. Computers will become better at processing videos and be able to more accurately identify individual people. They will also be more adept at finding behavioral patterns, such as someone loitering or acting in a strange manner. Also, a computer's ability to recognize objects such as bombs and guns should increase. Due to the threat of terrorism present in the world, it seems very plausible that scientists and computer engineers will uncover more technologies to curb terrorist threats due to an estimated high demand from law enforcement. This obviously raises fourth amendment issues. The legality of a search from a new piece of technology will of course depend on its pervasiveness in everyday society. The Supreme Court has said in *Kyllo v United States* that a device used to conduct a search in a home must be in everyday public use.[11] While some of the newer future technologies will most likely not be available for public use initially, some of the ones we have now will be. Technologies like GPS will be allowed to conduct searches. With an ever increasing amount of technology available to conduct searches, I believe the courts will more than likely start to categorize more activities as reasonable searches. As technology becomes more widely accepted and younger judges become appointed, people will become more accustomed to technology conflicting with our privacy rights. This familiarity will make the law more open to searches and seizures that today may seem unreasonable.

Another certain issue to be confronted will be technological warfare. I am becoming increasingly convinced that this will be the future battle zone for conducting wars. The damage that can be inflicted by one unbalanced individual with hacking skills is unsettling to say the least. Also, governments are becoming more adept at hacking into each other's mainframes and stealing valuable information. The Stuxnet virus is an example of the potential power a hacker has. The alarming thing is viruses and worms will become far more powerful in the not so distant future. More governments will emerge with legitimate hacking skills, and this will increase the amount of attacks everybody faces. With the increase of people and governments using powerful hacking techniques, the threat of a cyber attack becomes more possible and more potentially severe. There are thankfully positive trends happening in cyber law however in terms of preventing cyber attacks. As the talent of hackers advances, there will be an increase in demand for better security systems. Undoubtedly, with more people working on these security technologies, there will be many advances happening in the next thirty years. This poses a threat to our legal system in some ways. However, this is arguably more of a societal problem. It also will effect what constitutes an act of war.

Another thing I foresee is the phasing out of several positions and jobs that are currently manned by human beings. More jobs will be eliminated by technologies. For instance, I believe in the future that lawyers' jobs will become more technologically dependent. There will be more legal forms available online for people to complete themselves. There will also be new technologies in manufacturing that phase out jobs for human workers. This will create potential problems in labor law. In fact, it seems plausible that labor law will begin to lose significance in the legal realm. I believe that we will have to find different ways to create jobs for people. The increasing use of cheap, overseas labor will most likely continue to rise. Problems in international law and human rights will increase. Hopefully, as human rights awareness spreads around the world to developing countries, there will be fewer jobs exported to foreign nations.

One last technological innovation that could raise legal problems is the advances being made in car technology. Cars are able now to park themselves and avoid accidents. The problem I see with this is if we start losing more manual control of our vehicles, then what about accidents under tort law? It could be argued that if the car is parking itself, then it is not the driver's fault. This could transform tort law. I think the courts will still hold drivers responsible because it is their property, but the issue could arise and arguments would be made in its defense.

In thirty years, there will be a massive amount of technological innovations. This will affects many areas of law and continue to present challenging problems for our courts to litigate. As new and younger judges come onto courts, there will be a decrease in the sensitivity of technology in our lives. This will lead to courts becoming less adverse to technology influencing our daily lives.

---

[1] Kyllo v. United States, (313, 317)

Chapter 7

Baby Steps Into the Future: Technology in Society in 2040
Zachary Pratt

I.   Technology in the Year 2040

Predicting technological advances is a difficult endeavor to undertake. With the benefit of hindsight, one can look back on history and see a logical progression to how technology and communications have advanced. Patterns can also be discerned from this reflection, and rather than spew a 2011 version of the classic novel *1984*, it would be more prudent to study these patterns and apply them in looking towards the future.

For instance, the first e-mail was sent 40 years ago in 1971 using two terminals connected to a primitive form of the Internet.[1] Today, the choices for personal e-mail hosts seem infinite and business or student e-mail addresses are provided by virtually any organization that a person may belong to.

Another example of the systematic progression of technology would be the telephone. The first telephone call was made in 1876, and while the call was merely made by Alexander Graham Bell to another receiver within the same house, it wasn't until 1915 that a telephone in New York City could contact a receiver in San Francisco.[2] Once these capabilities were disclosed, telephones became commonplace in the household.

Furthermore, the television followed a very similar development cycle as the above mentioned devices. The first cathode-ray tube projector was first developed in 1907.[3] The Golden Age of Television, however, didn't begin until the early 1940s and lasted into the 1950s.[4]

In looking at these patterns, the most logical way of predicting what life will be like in thirty years will be to look at the cutting edge technology of today and expect that this technology will be the standard that will be adopted into the future. One instance of this is the video phone. On devices such as the iPhone 4™, the Samsung Galaxy Nexus™, or the LG Esteem™, a user can call another similar device using live video feeds similar to the technology used to communicate via webcam over the Internet. However, these devices all come with limitations, such as the need to have a Wi-Fi connection, the ability to only call similar devices, or the ability to only call another device on the same cellular network. This is one technology that could evolve over this time to the point that there will never be a phone call made without video also being sent.

Another cutting edge technology is the use of a computer system to control and monitor everything that is occurring in the user's home. Through advanced technology, one can access security systems, temperature controls, light switches, and any other electronic device that one can think of from thousands of miles away.[5] With the advances being made in this field, and the cost of using these products constantly decreasing, light switches, house keys, and thermostats could become a thing of the past. If all of these devices can be accessed from a single tablet PC or a cellular telephone, the hassle of controlling these things separately from different built-in devices would seem tedious.

The final major technological advancement that seems imminent is the availability of hologram communication. In early 2011, holograms became more than something that is seen in a science fiction movie when the University of Arizona developed a working, albeit primitive, hologram.[6] Over the next thirty years, this technology could become perfected to the point where it is marketable to an everyday citizen for a reasonable price. In 2040, we may be having three-dimensional hologram conversations in the same way that we have video conversations today.

The effect that this will have is that everything will be extremely centralized in our lives. As our technology advances and we have devices that can do more and more things, we become more dependent on these devices. Today, cell phones have the capability of doing more than just calling people. If the advances described above become the standard for society in 2040, it is completely possible that a singular device could become the sole way to contact others , control your home environment, unlocking the doors to your house or your car, start your car, give presentations at work, and any number of other things. A singular device could hold all of the identification material one would have, including digital copies of your social security card, driver's license, passports, birth certificate, wedding certificate, etc. This could even be extended to have that same device hold the identification information for your children or your spouse. As society becomes more dependent on these singular devices, they also become more protective of those devices and how freely they can use those devices, so regulating the extent that people can use these devices could be a tricky road for legislators to walk down as people eventually begin to take advantage of these devices and use the power for dastardly purposes.

II.   Policy Issues and How the Law Can Fix Them

The availability of such powerful devices in the hands of everyday citizens is eventually going to lead to problems that will need to be solved. If somebody's entire life resides in a singular computerized device, the temptation to gain access to a person's identity through hacking that device will be great. If a person's home is controlled by a centralized computer system, a criminal could find a way to hack into the person's home in order to burgle the home or to plant a virus into the system to cause different aspects of the house to be dangerously altered. Luckily, there is already a statute that can cover these policy issues, as the Computer Fraud and Abuse Act[7] already covers these issues. The usage of this statute would only have to be extended so that it would cover the new technology (which could be done by either re-interpreting the definitions in 18 U.S.C. §1030(e) or by altering the statute to include these new devices).

Another policy issue with the new devices would be with regards to obscenity laws. Today's courts have dealt with the laws of obscenity in regards to telephone calls, saying that instances where a person dials a telephone service with adult content (*i.e.*, Dial-A-Porn services) were not in violation of the law because of the affirmative actions one has to take in order to come across one of these services.[8] However, would the courts want to change their rulings as the capabilities of a phone increase? Images and videos usually have stronger restrictions than mere words and sounds, so the legality of a Dial-A-Porn service on video calls and hologram calls would likely need to be reviewed. However, these rules are likely to remain unchanged. There would still be a requirement that the user would need to take an affirmative action in contacting one of these services, and the increased technology may also bring on a way to easily confirm a user's age via the modernized devices. Regardless, the higher capabilities on a communication device lead to more opportunities for smut and obscene material to seep through the cracks and into the hands of those who would be harmed and offended by this material. The laws may need to get stricter based on this, but other technological advances (such as the age verification system) may make it so these stricter regulations are unnecessary.

Police monitoring and searches would also need to undergo a regulation overhaul. Would a police officer or federal institution hacking into your personal device constitute a search, and if so, what level of reasonableness would need to be present for that search to be legal? Could a police officer or federal institution hack into your home's computer system to inquire about any data or usage that is on the system, such as when you were in your home, when you left your home, how many people were in your home, or what activities are being conducted in your home? Could a police officer or federal institution be even more invasive, hacking into your home's computer to unlock the doors and suppress the security system so that they can walk into the home and conduct a search and seizure in the usual sense? These questions would be analyzed under court precedents, such as the police monitoring case using thermal scanners.[9] Courts ruled that the use of thermal scanners to obtain information regarding the inside of a person's home for a criminal investigation was wrongful without first obtaining a warrant and going through the typical process for searches and seizures.[10] Using this precedent, it seems that although this evidence would be much easier to obtain because of the ability to hack into a centralized device to obtain a multitude of information, courts would restrict police officers and federal institutions from accessing a person's devices or home computer without first going through the process of obtaining a search warrant for the specific evidence they are looking to find. The fact that the evidence is in a different medium should not alter the process that a government agency has to go through in order to obtain that information.

III.   Technology and Practicing Law

The art of practicing law has advanced incredibly with the advancement of technology. Instead of shouting loudly and precisely so that the judge, jurors, and observers could hear every word of a testimony, a courtroom is now more akin to a concert hall with microphones and speakers littered throughout.

Instead of rolling in mobile TVs to play video messages or evidence, some courts allow attorneys to play DVDs in a movie theatre-like atmosphere on a projection screen. With these advances becoming more of a standard rather than a privilege, it is reasonable to believe that even more technological advances will make their way into the courtroom.

Imagine a courtroom where every juror has their own personal monitor where they can see the evidence up close and the record is displayed like closed captioning on a television show. Imagine a judge who is given an iPad or some other tablet PC where he can scroll through the evidence given or go through the record in real time to easily rule on objections. Court documents can already be submitted online, but many systems could become much more efficient and the responses could be even quicker. Technology could become so powerful and reliable that witnesses could testify remotely. If the hologram technology is available, holographic evidence could be presented to court, showing scaled or exact dimensions of objects that cannot be brought into the court room.

Outside of the courtroom, the advancements of technology could still have profound effects. Libraries of statutes could be condensed to a single hard drive that is updated electronically rather than through expensive books. Client communication could become more efficient and more personalized. The added efficiency and the removal of high overhead costs could be reduced to the point where legal costs for a client could diminish without having to cut the pay of a lawyer. The entire legal profession would be overhauled, making it more accessible and more efficient.

IV.   Conclusion

Nobody can truly predict what technological devices will be prominent in the year 2040. If someone was able to predict this with enough certainty that they knew how it would be able to be produced, the technology would already be available. While developments in communication technology do come with their own policy problems and litigation issues, the benefits that this technology could bring will certainly make these landmark cases worth the trouble.

---

[1] http://openmap.bbn.com/~tomlinso/ray/ka10.html

[2] http://www.chevroncars.com/learn/history/history-telephone

[3] http://transition.fcc.gov/omd/history/tv/1880-1929.html

[4] http://transition.fcc.gov/omd/history/tv/1930-1959.html

[5] http://www.alarm.com/overview/mobile_access.aspx

[6] http://www.myfoxphoenix.com/dpp/news/only_on_fox/real-life-hologram-technology-1-21-2011

[7] 18 U.S.C. §1030

[8] *Sable Communications of California, Inc. v. FCC*, 543-547. Citation from 547.

[9] *Kyllo v. United States*, 313-319.

[10] Id.

Chapter 8

The Closing of the Internet
Martin Pyne

I am always hesitant to make bold predictions about the state of technology in the future. The best we can do from our necessarily fixed-in-time perspective is to extrapolate current trends and so foretell the future based on the present. Any truly bold innovation may put the lie to our tidy vision of the future. But philosophy aside, we live in an age where access to communications is fast becoming ubiquitous. The rise of the Internet has permitted easy access to information that would previously have required significantly more effort to obtain, whether it be news, entertainment, or simply chatting with friends. Recent developments in mobile computing have made it possible to spread this access to wherever one goes, while at the same time restricting the ability of users to install software. At the same time, the expansion of "social media" such as Twitter, Facebook, and Google+ have made it easier for a small number of websites to get a large quantity of people's time on the Internet. We must assume that these current trends will continue into the future.

The most recent and worrying trend that I have observed on the Internet is a regression of the more sprawling Internet of the early 2000s into one seemingly dominated by a few large websites. The most prominent example of this trend is Facebook. Facebook has about 150,000 users in the United States alone, and about 700 million worldwide.[1] Beyond simple features such as communications and sharing between its users, Facebook has introduced social games and other applications that keep users on Facebook and permit Facebook to gain even more information about its users. Recently, Facebook's "Open Graph" initiative encourages Facebook users to automatically share everything they read on other websites.[2] Google, the largest Internet search provider, also recently jumped into the social networking business with the launch of Google+. Both Facebook and Google encourage spending much of one's Internet time either on their sites or, using the "Like" or "+1" buttons, reporting back one's activities on the broader Internet.[3]

But the amount of data collected by Facebook, Google, and their ilk reveals far more about a person than they may realize. Both what an individual shares and what people close to them share can create a personality profile that may be quite specific. For instance, a 2009 MIT study could predict with 78% accuracy whether a given Facebook profile was of a gay male—and that study had to rely on information that the researchers could access.[4] Undoubtedly, plenty of profiling information, determined by site usage patterns, remains unavailable to the public but is used in determining which advertisements to serve to customers. While both private groups and public agencies have made efforts to stem online tracking, there is scant evidence that enough people care enough about their privacy for such measures to become widely used.[5] (Anecdotally, I've even heard fairly technology-savvy people praise the more targeted advertisements they receive by using a service like Gmail.)

The other major trend prevalent recently has been towards closed, less free systems for mobile use. The traditional desktop computer is one where the user can install the software of their choice. There are no restrictions on what one can install on one's own computer. By contrast, Apple, creator of the popular iPhone and iPad, allows only pre-approved applications, or "apps," to be installed on their devices. Apple's initial rejection of various applications, including those run by newsmagazines and a Pulitzer Prize-winning cartoonist, have raised censorship concerns.[6] Apple's primary competitor Google, developer of the Android mobile platform, while providing its own "Android Market," does permit the installation of third-party applications.[7] It remains to be seen whose vision of mobile computing wins out. While Google's Android had a majority of smart phone market share in the third quarter of 2011,[8] Apple's iOS makes the most money from application downloads.[9]

So what does this mean for the world of 2040? Unless there are truly egregious privacy violations that cause a widespread public outcry, I see most people accessing the Internet through the filters of social media sites and "apps" that limit both their ability to creatively contribute to the Internet at large and the content that they may access. While the rest of the Internet infrastructure will probably still exist, its users will be limited to those who possess the technological savvy and intellectual curiosity to visit it. To some extent, we see a possible parallel in Usenet. Popular before the rise of the World Wide Web, it is now mostly abandoned except for piracy purposes.[10] While the sheer breadth and depth of today's Web—and a user count much higher than Usenet even in its heyday—makes it unlikely that it will be abandoned to quite the same degree, it has already become much harder for a brand new site to become popular than it was a few years ago.[11] By 2040, the consolidation of the Internet—at least, the parts of it recognizable to us today—will have likely concluded.

I claim no ability to predict the political and legal climate of the next thirty years. A greater regulatory role by the Federal Communications Commission (FCC), Federal Trade Commission (FTC), or antitrust regulators could help forestall a narrower Internet. The push for "net neutrality" among legislators and policy advocates, which would ensure that network service providers do not favor some content providers over others, saw the 2010 enactment of FCC rules requiring some amount of net neutrality over physical lines.[12] However, these rules did not govern the wireless Internet, which is likely to be the most important area of network expansion in the next thirty years.[13] Attempts to establish net neutrality by Federal statute have failed in the face of Congressional opposition that is unlikely to dissipate any time soon.[14] Indeed, the most recent Congressional initiative on the Internet is the Stop Online Piracy Act, which both major Internet companies and public policy advocates oppose as an "internet blacklist bill".[15]

Ultimately, though, trying to address technological issues from a legal or political framework may be the wrong approach. The popularity of Facebook, Apple's mobile computing devices, and other systems that promote a "walled garden" user experience suggest that perhaps a less private, yet more controlled Internet is what most people actually want. If that truly is the case, then I fear the Internet of 2040 will be a more restrictive, less diverse place to exchange ideas than the Internet of 2011. While it may remain both legal and possible to visit the wilder, less impaired parts of the network and communicate outside of the dominant network paradigms, the law cannot force people to diversity their Internet habits. So the vast majority of Internet usage may well be confined to the safe, approved sites that one must use to communicate with almost anybody else, and the safe, approved applications that are publicized as the best vehicles for news and entertainment.

---

1   Christopher Williams, *Facebook Usage Drops in Britain and US*, THE TELEGRAPH, June 13, 2011,
http://www.telegraph.co.uk/technology/facebook/8573340/Facebook-usage-drops-in-Britain-and-US.html.

2   Molly Wood, *How Facebook is Ruining Sharing*, CNET NEWS (Nov. 18, 2011, 10:57 AM), http://news.cnet.com/8301-31322_3-57324406-256/how-facebook-is-ruining-sharing/.

3   *E.g.* Jared Newman, *Google +1 Now Links To Google Profiles: Let the War on Facebook's 'Like' Button Begin*, PCWORLD (Aug. 24, 2011, 1:15 PM), https://www.pcworld.com/article/238726/google_1_now_links_to_google_profiles_le t_the_war_on_facebooks_like_button_begin.html.

4   Steve Lohr, *How Privacy Vanishes Online*, N.Y. TIMES, Mar. 16, 2010, https://www.nytimes.com/2010/03/17/technology/17privacy.html (citing
Carter Jernigan & Behram F.T. Mistree, *Gaydar: Facebook Friendships Expose Sexual Orientation*, FIRST MONDAY (Oct. 5, 2009),
http://firstmonday.org/htbin/cgiwrap/bin/ojs/index.php/fm/article/view/2611/2302).

5   The latest initiative to this end is the "Do-Not-Track" header, which takes the form of a browser request to websites at the time the page is opened that the user does not want to be tracked. David Daw, *The State of 'Do Not Track' on the Internet*, PCWORLD (accessed Nov. 23, 2011); https://www.pcworld.com/article/223633/the_state_of_do_not_track_on_the_interne t.html. However, few seriously expect Congress to mandate that sites actually obey this header, so it is unlikely to stem tracking abuses. Tony Bradley, *Congress Takes Stab at 'Do Not Track' Legislation*, PCWORLD (accessed Nov. 23, 2011), https://www.pcworld.com/businesscenter/article/219815/congress_takes_stab_at_do _not_track_legislation.html.

6   Brian Stelter, *A Pulitzer Winner Gets Apple's Reconsideration*, N.Y. TIMES, Apr. 16, 2010, https://www.nytimes.com/2010/04/17/books/17cartoonist.html; Eric Pfanner, *Publishers Question Apple's Rejection of Nudity*, N.Y. TIMES, Mar. 14, 2010, https://www.nytimes.com/2010/03/15/technology/15cache.html.

7   *E.g.* Priya Ganapati, *Independent App Stores Take on Google's Android Market*,

Wired.com (June 11, 2010, 8:00 AM),
  http://www.wired.com/gadgetlab/2010/06/independent-app-stores-take-on-googles-android-market/.
8   Press Release, Gartner, Gartner Says Sales of Mobile Devices Grew 5.6 Percent in Third Quarter of 2011; Smartphone Sales Increased 42 Percent (Nov. 15, 2011), *available at* http://www.gartner.com/it/page.jsp?id=1848514.
9   Neil Hughes, *Google's Android Market Estimated to Earn Just 7% of What Apple's App Store Makes*, APPLEINSIDER (Nov. 21, 2011, 12:19 PM), http://www.appleinsider.com/articles/11/11/21/googles_android_market_estimated_to_earn_just_7_of_what_apples_app_store_makes.html.
10   *E.g.* Sascha Segan, *R.I.P Usenet: 1980-2008*, PCMAG.COM (July 31, 2008), http://www.pcmag.com/article2/0,2817,2326849,00.asp.
11   *See, e.g.,* Erik Loomis, *How to Succeed in Political Blogging*, LAWYERS, GUNS, AND MONEY (Nov. 8, 2011),
          http://www.lawyersgunsmoneyblog.com/2011/11/how-to-succeed-in-political-blogging ("[T]here's virtually no way for new voices to rise out of the blogosphere in 2011.).
12   Brian Stelter, *F.C.C. Is Set to Regulate Net Access*, N.Y. TIMES, Dec. 20, 2010, *https://www.nytimes.com/2010/12/21/business/media/21fcc.html.*
13 *Id.*
14   Matthew Lasar, *No Net Neutrality Plan from Congress, So Now What?*, ARS TECHNICA (Sept. 29, 2010, 7:29 PM),
  http://arstechnica.com/tech-policy/news/2010/09/no-net-neutrality-plan-from-congress-so-now-what.ars.
15   Dominic Rushe, *SOPA Condemned by Web Giants as 'Internet Blacklist Bill'*, THE GUARDIAN, Nov. 16, 2011,
  http://www.guardian.co.uk/technology/2011/nov/16/sopa-condemned-internet-blacklist-bill. As of this writing, the bill is pending before the House Committee on the Judiciary. H.R. 3261, 112th Cong. (2011).

Chapter 9

2040: What We Gained and What We Lost
Colby Steele

The chip in your head wakes you up, it's 6 a.m. and the start of another work day. You're thankful that you don't have to make breakfast anymore since your A.I. is already hard at work in the kitchen preparing breakfast for you. Your hologram TV turns on and tunes in exactly the channel your thoughts told it to. The nice thing about TV today is that it's not just your TV but also your computer, telephone, real-time utility usage reader and the best thing - it's foldable and portable! Furthermore, the advertising on your TV is only directed at you. In fact, these days the world seems centered around you. Communication is ubiquitous and instantaneous, and it's all for you. Ever since the government installed that chip in your head you have been linked to the most efficient and safe democracy in history, as well as, the most effective healthcare. The hospital is constantly reading your vital signs! Stem cell research has provided you with a new heart and lung and you feel better today than you did when you were 20 – back in 2011.

Of course, not only can the hospital read your vital signs -- but the government can now use your vital signs to judge, with 100% accuracy, if and when you'll commit a crime. The world today is safe. In fact, crime doesn't exist because people are caught before they can commit a crime. Trials to determine guilt or innocence are no longer needed because the mind-reading technology is 100% accurate and therefore automatically establishes proof beyond a reasonable doubt.[1]

Furthermore, your bank account is seamlessly linked to all the retailers in the world. You are no longer required to type in your address and credit card number when you buy something; you just click "buy." In fact, when you go grocery shopping you put all of the items in your basket and walk out of the store. On your way out, a scanner (located above the door) scans the items and immediately debits your bank account for the items in your basket. The same happens at the gas station and any other old-fashioned brick and mortar store that you may happen to visit. Life has never been easier or safer.

Your job as a virtual clutter organizer gets old sometimes because you just can't believe some of these data hoarders! They have all of their data and ancient files saved on thousands of one-terabyte external hard drives. You simply don't see any excuse for this type of behavior in an age of one exabyte (1 million terabytes) memory capacity! Thankfully, it has never been easier to transfer your skills into a new profession. There are many new professions in 2040. You could be an avatar manager, body part maker, cyber quarantine enforcer, social networking officer, vertical farmer, virtual lawyer or a memory augmentation surgeon.[2]

However, despite all of these "great" innovations you are one of the few who think you have given up too much to acquire the lifestyle you have now. As privacy gave way to positive externalities[3] the world gave way to consumerism. Social networking became the only social life we have and the government now knows every move you make, as well as every thought you have. An Illegal government search no longer exists in the United States because nobody has a subjective expectation of privacy that society thinks is reasonable.[4] Still, our First Amendment rights have never been stronger and our system of governance has never been more efficient.

Fourth Amendment: 2011 - 2040

The landmark case of *U.S. v. Jones*[5] can now be considered a major turning point in Fourth Amendment jurisprudential history. The police, CIA, FBI and DHS were given permission to bypass the process[6] of obtaining a warrant to constantly and continuously monitor the movements of citizens. People were told that we were safer (and we were) but no one calculated what we were giving up. Eventually, the populous no longer had a subjective expectation of privacy -- we surrendered privacy in the name of SAFETY.

In that same year, DHS began airing a public service announcement on the welcome screens of 1.2 million hotel room TVs[7]. DHS asked the public to be vigilant and report all suspicious activity to local authorities. The entire nation was deputized to work for the national government. We were all policing each other! Neighbors began spying on their neighbors and kids began spying on their parents. As discussed above, we no longer had Fourth Amendment protection from this type of constant surveillance.

In the height of Fourth Amendment protection, the person was protected along with the places they held private.[8] Now, we have a computer chip implanted in our skin next to our ear – in the name of safety. The subjective sense of privacy in one's home or person has faltered and now all Fourth Amendment litigation takes place only over encrypted data. Professional encrypting engineers are paid handsomely to encrypt data. However, once mind-reading technology advances, the problem will no longer exist because once you think about your encrypted data (or if a third party does) you have given the information to the government and therefore no longer have a legitimate right to privacy in that information.[9] Troubling.

First Amendment: 2011 – 2040

Protestors flooded the parks and sidewalks of cities throughout the nation. They held demonstrations and spoke against the government, big business and corruption. Eventually, as their movement gained strength, they were assaulted and inhumanely put down. At one camp, the police organized a nighttime raid. They carefully set up bright lights at the edge of the protestor's camp ground, dressed in full riot gear (shields, batons, pepper spray and guns) and at 2 a.m. turned on the bright lights in order to viciously beat the still sleeping protestors until they went home or were arrested. In other cities, peacefully protesting students were methodically sprayed with pepper spray – by their own campus police force. There was a great battle over First Amendment free speech. Who was protected and who wasn't? Was the speech indecent[10]? No. Was the speech obscene[11]? No. However, the government banned these protestors from the public parks using content neutral, time, place and manner regulations.[12]

A lawyer, who is a graduate of the University of Iowa College of Law, sought to enjoin the government from disbanding the protestors. He also wanted to prevent the government from denying the protestors their right to symbolic speech. He felt the protestors had a right to camp in public parks as a symbol of solidarity. The court in *Student 27 v. New York*, ruled in favor of the injunction. The court noted that under the *O'Brien* test[13] the state could not show a substantial government interest in not allowing the protestors to symbolically camp in public parks. Furthermore, the court said, that even if the government could show they had a substantial interest, they still were not regulating in the least restrictive means to further that interest. The Supreme Court granted certiorari and affirmed the district court's ruling. Protecting communication was the first step to revolution in this country and throughout the world.

Today, all speech is protected, *absolutely*[14], throughout the world. At about the same time as the Occupy protests in the USA, the United Kingdom, Australia, Canada and many others, the Arab Spring was occurring in the Middle East. This time in history saw corrupt government after corrupt government toppled by the freedom of speech and mass communication.[15] Freedom of speech united the world. All speech in today's cyberworld is protected because the internet's social norms, marketplace, architecture and governing body (ICANN) allow all speech to be presented to their appropriate audiences. [16] However, the right to speak anonymously has eroded along with our right to privacy.[17]

Cyber Regulation: 2011 – 2040

Looking back now, the problem with cyber regulation in 2011 was the internet's anonymity. The internet allowed millions of users to surf the web, behave poorly and join subversive groups[18] completely undetected. My class at the University of Iowa debated on whether or not east coast code[19] or west coast code[20] should be used to regulate the behavior of people online. We also discussed the internet's architecture, social norms and marketplace as possible checks on otherwise unidentifiable behavior. In 2011, people cared about their privacy in a way that we don't now due to the effects *U.S. v. Jones* (see, Fourth Amendment: 2011-2040) and its progeny. The idea of less privacy gave way to a combination of bottom up and top down regulation; a hybrid of east coast and west coast code mixed with the effective use of the internet's architecture by a regulatory body, ICANN.

ICANN was developed in the United States to provide order on the internet with regard to the task of assigning domain names. Now, it functions as the world's first cyberlaw governing body. After our individual sense of privacy eroded, the governments around the world argued about internet regulation as the internet had become its own "cybernation." Since then, privacy has given way to safety and this has allowed the governments around the world to devise an identification system to enforce their sovereign laws. Just as ICANN issued domain names, now all users must have an electronic user identification tag ("tag") in order to gain access to the internet. This tag contains pertinent information about each user, like our country of origin, the state (if applicable) we live in, our age, political associations, our criminal record and our user rating. However, most importantly, these tags are encoded with the laws of our nation and the laws of our particular state (if applicable). This code prohibits minors from viewing porn, buying alcohol etc… and allows adults to surf the web at their will and in accordance with their nation's laws. Each individual website is built with a macro that reads our particular tag and immediately reports our activity to a cyber quarantine robot that decides instantly whether or not our action is acceptable according to our nation's laws. The concept of the "tag" is the perfect example of east and west coast code working together.

Furthermore, in today's society nothing is more important to an individual than their user rating. Our user rating is a check on our behavior from our society – without government intervention. Your user rating can be inflated or deflated according with the general opinion about you within your cyber community. Your user rating operates similarly to your old credit score because it contains information from all of the same sources with the addition of your peers. People are no longer anonymous and therefore they seem to be acting more responsibly.

More importantly, laws have changed. In the past, property law[21], contract law[22] and tort law[23] governed cyber regulation. There was a debate with regard to the law of the horse.[24] However, the laws that govern cyberlaw today are those that are issued by ICANN. (ICANN User Agreement § 2832 listed in Appendix A). User agreements govern the way we interact online (along with our I.D. tag and user rating). In essence, statutory code and contract law proved to be the most effective way for ICANN to regulate online behavior. We are all bound by our user agreement with ICANN and furthermore with any website's user agreement with which we interact.

Life today is different than life in 2011. Personally, I think we have lost more in privacy than we have gained in the name of safety and efficiency.

---

[1] In Re Winship, 397 U.S. 358, 374 (1970)(citing C. McCormick, Evidence) – The doctrine of "beyond a reasonable doubt" was applied in courts before mind reading technology existed. If a defendant didn't admit guilt he was given a trial to determine guilt or innocence by his peers (a jury). This doctrine is no longer applied today because guilt is established by our thoughts.

[2] Emerging Job Titles of Today, 2030 – 2039 Timeline Contents, http://www.futuretimeline.net/21stcentury/2030-2039.htm (listing numerous new professions that could be available to the public in the year 2039).

³ The concept that as a network gets the larger its value also increases. In 2040, positive externalities have been very important to DHS, CIA, FBI and other similar policing organizations. The more people they have registered in their networks, the safer we all are. This concept also applies to commercial entities.

⁴ Kyllo v. United States, 121 S. Ct. 2038 (2001) (explaining the jurisprudential standard of determining a violation of the 4th Amendment in 2001 - 39 years ago).

⁵ United States v. Jones, 131 S. Ct. 3064 (2011) (holding in favor in of allowing warrantless GPS tracking (6-3) and the erosion of subjective privacy quickly began).

⁶ Katz v. United States, 88 S. Ct. 507 (1967)(explaining that judicial safeguards protect the citizen from their government and unreasonable search and seizures).

⁷Barbara De Lollis, Hotel Guests Recruited with Homeland Security TV Spots, USA Today Travel, http://travel.usatoday.com/hotels/story/2011-11-02/Hotel-guests-recruited-with-Homeland-Security-TV-spots/51032602/1. This piece from USA Today depicts the first of many public service announcements aimed at the general public by the United States Government.

⁸ Katz, 88 S. Ct. at 511-12 (protecting a man from being wiretapped while in a telephone booth).

⁹ United States v. Miller, 96 S. Ct. 1619 (1976)(sharing communication with with a 3rd party puts the speaker or writer at risk that that information may be revealed to the government by the 3rd party).

¹⁰ FCC v. Pacifica, 98 S. Ct. 3026 (1978)(holding that indecent speech receives restricted1st Amendment protection - not absolute protection).

¹¹ Roth v. United States, 77 S. Ct. 1304 (1957)(holding obscenity does not receive 1st Amendment protection).

¹² Renton v. Playtime Theaters, Inc., 106 S. Ct. 925 (1986)(explaining that content neutral speech regulation is ok as long as it serves a substantial government interest and does not unreasonably limit alternative avenues of communication).

¹³ United States v. O'Brien, 88 S. Ct. 1673 (1968)(describing a test for symbolic speech – noting that the law that regulates speech must be within the constitutional power of the government to act, the regulation must further a substantial government interest, the suppression must be content neutral, and the regulation must prohibit no more speech than is essential to further the substantial government interest).

¹⁴ As discussed above, in the United States the freedom of speech was only if it was not obscene or indecent – and in 2011 New York City Mayor Michael Bloomberg declared that no right to free speech was absolute! Mark Memmot, New York Police Clear Occupy Wall Street Protestors From Park, The Two-way, http://www.npr.org/blogs/thetwo-way/2011/11/15/142336656/new-york-police-clear-occupy-wall-street-protesters-from-park. Today, the right to free speech is absolute.

¹⁵ Iyadelbaghdadi, Meet Asmaa Mahfouz and The Vlog That Helped Spark the Revolution, http://www.youtube.com/watch?v=SgjIgMdsEuk. (showing a video of Asmaa Mahfouz – she was famous in 2010 for starting the protests in Egypt).

¹⁶ Patricia L. Bellia et al., Cyberlaw: Problems of Policy and Jurisprudence in the Information Age 11 (4th ed. 2010)(discussing Lawrence Lessig's law of the horse and the constraints of control (1) laws, (2) norms, (3) markets and (4) architecture).

¹⁷ Patricia L. Bellia et al., Cyberlaw: Problems of Policy and Jurisprudence in the Information Age 394 (4th ed. 2010). In 2011 courts recognized a right to freedom of

speech that included anonymous speech. Today, speech is produced instantaneously online with the author's I.D. tag issued by ICANN. There is no threat of economic or social retaliation because all action is instantaneously reported. In a world of instant communication it's hard to get by with poor behavior.

[18] One such group was a loosely affiliated group of hackers called, Anonymous. Today, the group no longer exists because every user's activity is linked to their I.D. chip. Elinor Mills, Israeli Government Sites Down After Anonymous Threat, CNET News, http://news.cnet.com/8301-1009_3-57319767-83/israeli-government-sites-down-after-anonymous-threat/?tag=txt;title (telling the story of one of the many Anonymous action plans).

[19] East coast code is the slang term my class chose to apply to legislatively enacted laws and statutes.

[20] West coast code is the term we used to denote computer code – the code that restricts or enhances our ability to use a certain function on the computer

[21]Intel Corp. v. Hamidi, 71 P.3d 296 (Cal. 2003). Intel attempts to assert a property claim against a former employer and spammer who sent tens of thousands of unsolicited emails to current Intel employees describing Intel's poor hiring practices.

[22]ProCD, Inc. v. Zeidenberg, 86 F.3d 1447 (7th Cir. 1996). A company successfully held a consumer to their contract that was not physically displayed. Additionaly, in America Online v. LCGM, 46 F. Supp. 2d 444 (E.D. Va. 1998), America Online was able to enforce their user agreement (which prohibited spam) on users who acknowledged accepting the agreement.

[23]Zeran v. America Online, Inc., 129 F.3d 327 (4th Cir. 1997)(involving anonymous defamatory speech and the problems it presents for ISP's and 3rd parties)

[24]Patricia L. Bellia et al., Cyberlaw: Problems of Policy and Jurisprudence in the Information Age 4-11 (4th ed. 2010). The law of the horse was a school of thought first introduced by Judge Frank Easterbrook that believed cyberlaw had to be governed by a form of law that already existed. He believed cyberlaw was best governed by already existing law similar to the "law of the horse." Lawrence Lessig pointed out that the law of the horse idea was not necessarily true because cyberspace involved much more than the normal categories of law. It involved code, architecture, social norms and a vibrant marketplace. Lessig suggested that all four of these components must be used in order to regulate cyberspace effectively. It turns out that neither of them were completely right.

Chapter 10

Privacy 3.0 : The Human Information Device Exchange
Allison K. VanNatta

Coffee Shop
Good morning, Mr. Smith. Will you be having your standard coffee this morning?
Response: Yes. Swipe it.

Taxi Cab
Good morning, Mr. Smith. Am I taking you to your office this morning?
Response: Yes. Swipe it.

The Office
Good morning, Mr. Smith. Are you just getting here this morning?
Response: Yes. Swipe it.

Doctor's Appointment
Good morning, Mr. Smith. Are you seeing the doctor this afternoon? And may I have your updates insurance information?
Response: Yes. Swipe it.

Surfing the Web
Website visited: www.obscenity.xxx
Message embodied in pop-up window upon entering site: Welcome, Mr. Smith!

I.   The Human Information Device Exchange ("HIDE")
Swipe it. This terminology will not mean the same thing today as it will in 2040. Today, this phrase is most commonly used in reference to one's usage of a credit or debit card and it represents what we, as people of 2011, think of as some of our most convenient means of associating in society. However, this concept will be comical to individuals living in 2040 because its convenient nature will not compare to the technology of 2040, known as the Human Information Device Exchange ("HIDE"). The HIDE chip is a small piece of software surgically embedded into the arm of human beings. It has many capabilities and its versatility can best be described by walking through the daily activities of the aforementioned Mr. Smith. First, we see the original convenience of the credit/debit card phenomenon taken to a new level. The HIDE chip technology allows an individual to link his or her bank account to the device's software and allows purchases to be made simply by swiping the

arm housing the device. This new level of convenience removes the need for any physical carrying of credit cards or accompanying identification materials. Although this feature may seem innovative to generations of 2011, it will ultimately prove to be the least complex feature offered.

The second activity of Mr. Smith involved him taking a taxi to work. Based on the conversation alone, it may appear that Mr. Smith uses his HIDE device to simply perform the same function as his coffee purchase mentioned above. However, what you cannot tell from the conversation transcript alone is that the there is no human asking Mr. Smith questions. The taxi cab is operated by a robot and as soon as Mr. Smith enters the vehicle, a list of routes recently traveled becomes available on a computer screen on the taxi computer.[1] The third activity involved Mr. Smith arriving at work. Upon arrival, his HIDE device performs two pre-programmed tasks. First, it sends Mr. Smith's secretary an email letting him know that he has arrived in the building. Second, it officially clocks him into work, meaning that it begins calculating the number of hours he will work that day. At the end of the day, his HIDE device then clocks him out of work and sends an email to his superior with a tabulation of the amount of hours he worked.

The two final activities of Mr. Smith's day further illustrate the capabilities of this new device. After work, Mr. Smith goes to his doctor's appointment. Upon arrival, he does not sign in on a piece of paper or read his name aloud to the secretary. Instead, he swipes his HIDE device and all of his personally identifiable information comes up on the screen for the secretary, including his name, address, phone number, health history, prescription list, and insurance data. After leaving the doctor's office, Mr. Smith goes home and gets on the Internet. He visits www.obscenity.xxx, a website containing obscene materials which, by 2040, is prohibited to anyone 18 years or younger. After typing in the URL, the website sends a signal to Mr. Smith's HIDE which in turn sends a signal back to the website confirming Mr. Smith's identity and acknowledging that he is of the legal age limit. If Mr. Smith were to walk away from the computer, the website would discontinue working until another HIDE device confirmed a signal that the user was of the appropriate age. The HIDE software is capable of sending various signals to websites, allowing individuals to purchase items, log-in without manually typing in a password, or download certain information into an email.

Privacy 3.0 – **A Need for New Ideas**

The HIDE technology will force evolution in several areas, including our lives, our laws, and our careers. Looking at the progression of judicial decisions and legislation, it is no secret that the law fails to adequately balance individual rights of privacy and technological advances as they happen.[2] One can get a better understanding of this imbalance by looking to the legislative and judicial responses to telephone technology in the 1940's and the 1960's. In *Olmstead*, the Supreme Court stated that an individual installing a telephone in his home intended to "project his voice to those quite outside." Nearly forty years later, the Court recognized that it misunderstood the technology and its relationship with people using it.[3] The HIDE is likely to create the same progression of technological and judicial confusion.

The biggest concerns likely to emerge with technological advances all surround one legal concept, the Fourth Amendment right to privacy. This is true because the vast majority of technology created between 2011 and 2040 will inevitably focus on tracking people in their every move. As of 2011, this tracking feature plays an essential role in the functionality of cellular phones, social media networks such as Facebook, and advertisements targeting individuals based on their movement.[4] While the HIDE device has storage capabilities, its primary purpose will be tracking everything from health data to places traveled to websites frequented. The key attraction to individuals will be its convenience and, as we already have learned from the public sharing exhibited on social media, people are more than willing to forfeit privacy interests in the name of quicker or more contemporary technologies. Some legal scholars categorize privacy problems as being Privacy 1.0 – focusing on inadvertent disclosures - or Privacy 2.0 – focusing on data collection and peer exchanges.[5] The HIDE device will create problems that cannot be resolved by applying the remedies to Privacy 1.0 or 2.0. In fact, the legal community will need to unite to create a remedy to Privacy 3.0. In 1996, Easterbrook hinted at a strategy for harmonizing the law and technology by stating that we do not understand the evolving world well and that we should "do what is essential to permit the participants in this evolving world to make their own decisions."[6]

Judicial Responses: Two Predetermined Spheres and a Gray Area

Much of the Fourth Amendment jurisprudence dealing with the right to privacy can be categorized into two separate spheres, that which relates to the home, and that which relates to information known to the public.[7] The HIDE device will force the law to recognize and evaluate yet another sphere created by its technology, involving information on the HIDE that is not necessarily within the confines of the home but not necessarily publicly available either. For example, the HIDE not only tracks a current route traveled in a car, but stores all previously traveled routes as well. Based on previous theories of law, that information could arguably be considered to have been shared with a third party, therefore making it public.[8] On the other hand, some theories would suggest that the HIDE chip holder would have a reasonable expectation of privacy.[9]

Because all of the gray areas cannot be clarified within the confines of this paper, the black letter law regarding the two spheres involving the home and public will be discussed and a few of the "gray areas" falling within the third sphere will be addressed. First, the information found to pertain to activity within the home will be protected by the Fourth Amendment and will therefore require a warrant to obtain.[10] Second, the information found to pertain to activity generally available to the public will not be protected by the Fourth Amendment.[11] In Justice Harlan's concurrence to the *Katz* decision, he stated that "objects, activities, or statements" exposed to the "plain view of outsiders" are not protected because the actor in question made no effort to privatize the information.[12] The HIDE chip will implicate employment settings, healthcare privacy rights, financial security, and public authority access to information and/or evidence of criminal defendants. Our previous jurisprudence paves the way for an illustration of how the courts in 2040 will treat information falling outside the limits of spheres one and two. Unfortunately, it is more than likely that the courts will not handle this sphere properly, based on the judicial patterns studied by this course.

What I think the courts will do is not necessarily what I think the courts *should* do. I think that they will fail in four respects: (1) by attempting to categorize all HIDE information into home or public spheres; (2) by focusing too heavily on societal norms; (3) by ignoring individual expectations of privacy; and (4) by triggering the third party default rule finding information shared with a third party to not be considered private. In 2040, the courts will find that data on the HIDE which is voluntarily shared with a third party is not protected by the Fourth Amendment.[13] The HIDE chip will consistently be sharing data with third parties to allow the device users to purchase items, use certain websites, or check in at a healthcare facility. The data will get judicial treatment analogous to that given to email communications in the 21st Century.[14] The courts will therefore interpret the fact that the HIDE device generates data output to third parties as waiving any Fourth Amendment protection to that data.

What I think the courts should do is recognize that this type of technology is not simply a difference in degree from the technology of 2011, but a difference of kind. Therefore, old principles stemming from telephones and standard emails cannot be applied. Instead, all of the information contained on the device should be protected by the Fourth Amendment, including bank account information, health history, and places visited. This type of treatment will allow individuals to participate in cutting-edge technology without being forced to forfeit constitutional rights.

II.   The Practice of Law: A Unified Effort to Draw Attention to Individual Interests

Because the court system will inevitably fail to treat the HIDE chip in such a way that appropriately balances the privacy interests of individuals against technological advances, the practice of law must be shaped to encourage the constitutional protections of that imbalance. Therefore, practitioners must be creative in crafting causes of action with one goal in mind, drawing attention to the individual expectations of privacy and reiterating that old principles of law must evolve to adequately address the gray areas.[15] Attorneys will need to focus on fact-finding techniques that allow them to demonstrate to the judges not only how the technology works, but also how people associate with that technology. Specifically, they will need to demonstrate the overarching benefits of convenience and practicality embodied in the HIDE and show that the law can change to protect individual interests. The relationship between users and the device will shape the way they live their lives and the way the world functions. It will therefore also inevitably affect the law. As the example above demonstrates, Mr. Smith relies on his HIDE chip to purchase items, store personally identifiable information, and assist him in creating convenience in his lifestyle. Focusing on this technological relationship will create a uniform effort among practitioners aimed towards making the judiciary recognize that the HIDE is not something that merely is a difference in degree, but rather is a difference in kind.

---

[1] By the year 2040, I firmly believe that cars will no longer be driven by human beings, but rather by internal systems similar to a robot. The issues surrounding this innovation within technology cannot efficiently be addressed in a paper of this length, and therefore will not be analyzed in terms of public policy or legal ramifications.

[2] Olmstead v. United States, 277 U.S. 438, found in *Cyberlaw* page 306, holding that wire taps on telephone lines did not violate the Fourth Amendment rights of individuals.

[3] Katz v. United States, 389 U.S. 347, found in *Cyberlaw* page 309, holding that wire taps on telephone lines were in fact a search and seizure, therefore overruling *Olmstead*.

[4] Sam Kiley, "Smartphone Spyware Software Tracks Every Move," found at http://news.sky.com/home/technology/article/16099260; Taylor Hatmaker, "New wristband Tracks Your Every Move in the Name of Health," found at http://news.yahoo.com/blogs/technology-blog/wristband-tracks-every-move-name-health-021044019.html.

[5] Jonathan Zittrain, *The Future of the Internet – and How to Stop It*, pp. 203-215, Yale University Press (2008), found in *Cyberlaw* 700, 702. As Zittrain points out, new "generative uses of the Internet" made solutions proposed for Privacy 1.0 inapplicable. Therefore, new solutions are required for Privacy 2.0. This demonstrates the generational gap in technology.

[6] Frank H. Easterbrook, *Cyberspace and the Law of the Horse*, 1996 U. Chi. Legal. F. 207, found in *Cyberlaw* 4, 6.

[7] Olmstead, found in *Cyberlaw* page 306; Katz, found in *Cyberlaw* page 309; Kyllo, 533 U.S. 27 found in *Cyberlaw* page 313; Warshak v. United States, 490 F.3d 455, vacated on reh'g en banc, 532 F.3d 521 found in *Cyberlaw* page 320; Smith v. Maryland, 442 U.S. 735; Berger v. New York, 388 U.S. 41.

[8] Warshak v. United States, found in *Cyberlaw* page 320, citing United States v. Jacobsen, 466 U.S. 109 found in *Cyberlaw* page 323.

[9] Warshak v. United States, found in *Cyberlaw* page 320, citing United States v. Miller, 425 U.S. 435 found in *Cyberlaw* 323.

[10] Katz, found in *Cyberlaw* page 309, 310.

[11] Id., J. Harlan concurring, found in *Cyberlaw* page 312, stating that "Thus a man's home is, for most purposes, a place where he expects privacy, but objects , activities, or statements that he exposes to the plain view' of outsiders are not protected because no intention to keep them to himself has been exhibited."

[12] Id.

[13] In Warshak, the Supreme Court struggled with the concept of access to email content versus email subscriber information, finding that if an Internet Service Provider notified the subscriber that the content of its emails would be accessed, no expectation of

privacy existed. Warshak, found in *Cyberlaw* 320, 326.

[14] United States v. Heckenkamp, found in *Cyberlaw* 326-327; United States v. Simons, found in *Cyberlaw* 326.

[15] Legal scholars point out that the law and technology are much like the analogy between the tortoise and the hare. Easterbrook points out that "Error in legislation is common and never more so than when the technology is galloping forward." Frank H. Easterbrook, *Cyberspace and the Law of the Horse*, 1996 U. Chi. Legal. F. 207, found in *Cyberlaw* 4, 6.

Chapter 11

Faster, Smarter, and Indispensable:
Legal Implications of an Increasingly Powerful and Vulnerable Communications System

Sam Young

By 2040, computing power will be exponentially more powerful than it is today. Advances in "smart" technology will fundamentally change the way humankind works, governs, transacts business, and interacts. Importantly, the utility of these emerging technologies will rest not only on the discrete power of individual devices, but also (and perhaps to a greater extent) on a given device's ability to communicate with other devices. The benefits of these ultra-smart, ultra-connected communications devices will be numerous: as the quality, speed, and "intelligence" of computing devices increase, individuals and organizations of all sizes will become better educated and better adept at facing the challenges of the future. However, humankind's reliance on such technologies will also come at a price. As more and more of civilization's vital interests are placed "online" and communicated electronically, the more vulnerable we will become to attacks on these networks and, relatedly, the more vulnerable we will become to government intrusions on our privacy. This paper will explore the likely developments in communications that the world will see by 2040, and will address several legal implications that will follow.

I.   Developments in Technology and Communications

Moore's Law holds that computing power will double every two years.[1] Relatedly, as computing power increases, the cost of computing power decreases: thus, today's computing power will be available for half its current cost two years from now.[2] Experts believe that these trends will continue at least through 2020, while thereafter the growth may slow to a doubling every three years.[3] If even conservative estimates hold true, by 2040 computing power will be tens of thousands of times more powerful than it is today, at a fraction of the cost.

Applying Moore's Law, 30 years from now we can expect the following: 1) the computing power of today's supercomputers will be available in modest personal computing devices; 2) the supercomputers of 2040 will have exponentially more power than today's supercomputers; and 3) the costs of such computing power will decline in rough proportion to the growth in computing power. These developments will have an incredible effect on human communications. By 2040, computers will be able to instantly and perfectly respond to complex verbal or written human queries. The rational first resource for virtually any human inquiry, whether personal, professional, theoretical, etc., will no longer be one's fellow human, but one's inexpensive, incredibly powerful, and highly connected computing device. Connected with other devices, including supercomputers exponentially more powerful than those of 2011, these devices will collect, store, and communicate incredible amounts of data, and will use this ever-increasing bank of knowledge to better serve the needs of their users.[4]

A. Access

One important consequence of all these developments will be that access to communications networks will come to be viewed as a basic necessity. Given the ever increasing abilities of computers (and their decreasing costs), vast numbers of jobs will be eliminated as smart technologies become cost-feasible alternatives to human employees. Those jobs that will remain will almost certainly require technical training and education, both of which by 2040 will require access to communications networks. Additionally, given the vast wealth of information these networks will possess, and the increasing ability of smart devices to answer important questions regarding health, science, and so on, those unable to afford access to communications will be at a great disadvantage.

Therefore, by 2040 I anticipate Congress will have passed a federal law creating an individual right of affordable access to communications networks. This right will be achieved in one of two ways: either by the government constructing a nationwide network available for free to all citizens, or by requiring private communications companies to provide low-cost or no-cost access to needy individuals. When faced with a choice between these options, communications companies will likely acquiesce to the latter.

Legal support for this "universal right of access" can be found in numerous sources. First, cases such as *Red Lion* introduce the concept that the government can impose obligations on communications companies as a condition of licensure.[5] Thus, communications companies who operate under government licensure, and who enjoy the use of government land and airways to support their networks, may be compelled to provide access as a condition of their operation. Second, in an environment where access to such networks represents a fundamental right, the denial of access may be prohibited under the Due Process and/or Equal Protection Clauses of the Constitution.[6] For while communications companies may be private companies, the services they provide can be viewed as quasi-public in nature, and thus subject to the requirements of the Constitution. If denying access to poor or remotely located citizens effectively denies such citizens equal access to essential services, such denial may violate their constitutional rights.

B. Security & Privacy

These communications, from humans to devices, devices to other devices, and devices back to humans will be the cornerstone of human interaction by 2040. As computing power grows in the coming decades, not only individuals but government, defense, industry, utilities, and other vital national concerns will become increasingly dependent on communications networks to function efficiently and effectively. Unfortunately, as this dependence grows, so too will the incentive of cyber criminals—some state-sponsored—to attack these networks. Therefore, a key communications issue in 2040 will be protecting communications from foreign interception, appropriation, and destruction.

As even the staunchest of libertarians will agree, a government has a duty to protect its citizens from external threats. Historically, meeting this duty has entailed building up defenses to physical threats, such as armies, militants, or destructive devices. While physical threats will continue to exist in the decades to come, by 2040 the threat posed by cyber-attacks will be equally severe. As articulated by John McConnell, and as fictionally depicted in Hollywood films, "fire sale" attacks are even today within the realm of the possible. Government participation in cyber-espionage and cyber-attacks, as evidenced in Operation Shady Rat[7] and the Stuxnet episode,[8] will continue to escalate. Therefore, if the government is to succeed in defending its population from foreign cyber-attack in 2040, it must engage in rigorous cyber-defense activities.

Recent news articles have reported that even today the NSA is reaching out to domestic public utilities, financial institutions, and defense contractors to assist them in building defenses against cyber-attacks.[9] In light of the dangers posed by state-sponsored cyber-attacks, this development might be viewed as encouraging. However, it also begs the questions: will such state involvement grant the government access to data on U.S. citizens? If so, is such access constitutional? And if not should it be, given the dire consequences of a successful cyber-attack?

The answers to these questions are likely yes, no, and a qualified yes. As the government increases its role in defending our infrastructure from cyber-attacks, to be effective it will likely have to monitor communications patterns and data. At some level this might merely entail collecting data regarding IP addresses, dates, times and so forth, which poses less of a constitutional problem than searching a communication's content.[10] However, as the costs of data storage becomes increasingly *de minimis*, it is likely that content will in many instances be at least stored, and perhaps accessed, as part of cyber-defense activities. This would constitute an unconstitutional invasion of privacy in so far as these searches and seizures violate the public's reasonable expectation of privacy and the Fourth Amendment.

The real question then is how to balance the need for effective cyber-security against the protections of the Fourth Amendment and other constitutional protections. My fear is that it will take just one serious cyber-attack, similar in scope to a 9/11 event, to create sufficient panic amongst voters and politicians to essentially obliterate the Fourth Amendment protections against unreasonable (warrantless) searches and seizures of communications data. Therefore, it is imperative that in the decades to come politicians address the threat cyber-attacks pose during a time of peace, and not in the aftermath of a crisis. To be frank, granting the government an enhanced role in protecting our cyber-infrastructure may require giving up some privacy rights. The key, however, is to approach this problem rationally and transparently, and with ample input from legal, technological, and industry experts.

To achieve an optimal balance between providing effective cyber-defense on the one hand and maintaining privacy interests on the other, Congress must develop legislation that carefully outlines the limits of government data collection and communications monitoring activities. Consistent with the opinions in *Katz*,[11] *Kyllo*,[12] and *Warshak*,[13] Congress (and the courts) must recognize that even if there are compelling state interests for invading a person's privacy, citizens are entitled to some modicum of privacy in their communications. Therefore, even if the government is granted heightened monitoring powers, it is important that these powers remain subject to judicial scrutiny. Further, the public should be informed regarding the extent to which their communications are protected from government monitoring.

If properly and proactively managed by both the legislative and judicial branches, the year 2040 may yet see an acceptable balance between privacy and security, allowing the incredible advances in communications technologies now on the horizon to benefit civilization at a minimal cost to our liberties.

---

[1] Steve Hassett, *Technology on the Horizon: What if Moore's Law Continues for Another 40 Years?*, SEEKING ALPHA (Oct. 6, 2010),
http://seekingalpha.com/article/228663-technology-on-the-horizon-what-if-moores-law-continues-for-another-40-years. Similarly, an iPhone costing $600.00 today can be expected to sell for about $0.25 in 2040.

[2] *Id.*

[3] *Id.*

[4] Even in 2011, the cost of data storage is falling dramatically, especially as computing needs are migrated to the cloud. See Clint Boulton, Google Storage Price Cuts Show Cloud is Competitive, Maturing, eWeek.com (Nov. 12, 2011),
http://www.eweek.com/c/a/Data-Storage/Google-Storage-Price-Cut-Shows-Cloud-is-Competitive-Maturing-377061/.

[5] Red Lion Broadcasting Co. v. FCC, Casebook 207, 209.

[6] See generally, William Cohen, CONGRESSIONAL POWER TO INTERPRET DUE PROCESS AND EQUAL PROTECTION (1975) (for general discussion of Due Process and Equal Protection Rights as they relate to Congressional legislation).

[7] CEL Class Reading Assignment: Dmitri Alperovitch, "Revealed: Operation Shady RAT," MCAFEE (2011).

[8] CEL Class Discussion; and William J. Broad, *Israeli Worm Called Crucial in Iran Nuclear Delay*, N.Y. TIMES (Jan. 15, 2011),
http://www.nytimes.com/2011/01/16/world/middleeast/16stuxnet.html?pagewanted=all.

[9] Aliya Sternstein, *Corporate Intelligence*, NEXTGOV: TECHNOLOGY AND THE BUSINESS OF GOVERNMENT (Nov. 2, 2011),
http://www.nextgov.com/nextgov/ng_20111102_7412.php?oref=topnews.

[10] Warshak v. United States, Casebook 320.

[11] Katz v. United States, Casebook 309, 309.

[12] Kyllo v. United States, Casebook 313, 313.

[13] Warshak v. United States, Casebook 320, 320.

Chapter 12

Regulating Big Brother

Anonymous 1

I.   Introduction

In the past 30 years, we have witnessed a revolutionary explosion in communications technology. Having reached this stage, the next 30 years will likely build on the advancements we have already made, and we can expect an evolution of existing trends in Internet and technology use. This paper will speculate on the legal and policy impact of improved artificial intelligence capability as it is incorporated in personal communication devices and private and government surveillance technology.

II.   Technological Innovations based on Artificial Intelligence

As the computational power of computers increased in the 1990s and into the 2000s, Artificial Intelligence ("AI") capability has been able to be used for data mining, logistics, and medical diagnosis. At its full potential, machines employing general intelligence (or strong AI) will be able to utilize many functions of the human brain, such as reasoning, assimilation of knowledge, planning, communication, learning based on observation and accumulated experience, and perception. I believe that the next 30 years will bring AI capability a step closer to its full potential, but not to the level of general intelligence. In 2040, cell phones will be almost entirely replaced by smartphones, and Internet accessibility will increase and become cheaper. With higher-powered smart phones in daily use, there will be a larger market for programs developed with AI capability. We are seeing precursors to this development today in the iPhone's "Siri." Although not technically empowered by AI, Siri is able to respond to an iPhone user's questions asked in colloquial English through identifying a set of words and outputting data on the basis of those words.[1] The advent of responsive machines like Siri has launched a movement towards increased human interaction with and reliance on machines and their efficient information gathering and processing capability. Once machines are able to intelligently analyze assimilated information and make human-like decisions, the existing trend of machine-human interaction will increase and expand.

This section will explore the implications of a few possible technological innovations that are likely to emerge by 2040: 1) Equivalent versions of Siri in all smartphones with human mood-sensing capability based on AI, and 2) improved private and government surveillance utilizing AI.

The first possible technological innovation would enable smartphone users to make requests for a variety of information through a program, but the program will be able to analyze and choose information on the basis of the user's preferences, personality, and even present mood. User requests could range from decisions on what to wear based on the weather, what to purchase for a winter wardrobe, what to eat to feel more energized, what exercise routine to use that day, what new music to purchase, and even which college to attend. This AI-based program will incorporate elements of game theory, decision theory, and perception skills to detect emotions in order to offer an answer to the requested information catered to the user's personality. The program will have the benefit of being able to access information on the Internet and organize all information related to the request, which will make its decision-making process more informed than the average human's decision-making process. With a few initial inputs from the user about themselves and a "learning" capability, the program will continue to learn more about the user throughout their request-answer relationship, similar to how human beings come to know one another after prolonged interaction and observation.

A second possible technological innovation would build on a trend that is already happening today: development of intelligent video surveillance devices. In 2040, video surveillance capability will have advanced to enable unmanned cameras to store and process information from several cameras and databases at once to assess potential security threats, and bring attention to relevant authorities once a threat is identified. Cameras empowered with AI will have the capability to discern what is mundane activity and what is potentially dangerous, like a human brain, but will have the benefit of processing past stored surveillance and all current surveillance. In assessing what is potentially dangerous, the cameras could employ mood-sensing technology to assess heart rate and other indicators of anxious movement. Unlike humans, the cameras will not need breaks or vacation time. The cost-effectiveness of such technology will give government and private actors incentives to install cameras in a wide variety of public and private places. By linking geographic movement of people and transportation to private and governmental data, such as the license plate numbers of stolen cars, car insurance records, or fingerprint data of wanted criminals, cameras will be able to assist in the prosecution of crimes previously committed in addition to investigating contemporaneous crimes.

III.   General Impact of Technology and Impact on the Practice of Law

Machines enabled with AI will have a significant impact on our society in 2040. With regards to the smartphone program discussed above, businesses would likely seek to encourage the use of such technology, paying for the advertisement of their services to correlate with certain consumer preferences or moods. Businesses would highly value having access to AI empowered programs that can provide extremely accurate measures of consumer preferences. In terms of cultural impact, becoming more and more dependent on machines for daily decision-making will take a toll on independent creative thinking, and also on interpersonal relationships. Although technology will provide numerous outlets for self-expression, increased interconnectedness with the rest of world will lead to further conflation of cultural preferences across the globe, a trend which is already underway.

Intelligent surveillance will likely lead to greater accuracy in criminal investigation and prosecution, but may lead to unreasonable government intrusion and have a chilling effect on speech and freedom of association protected by the First Amendment, depending on the law's response to such surveillance. In urban areas, equally distributed surveillance may help address the current disparate interaction that minority communities have with law enforcement, due to the over policing of residentially segregated areas. However, if government surveillance reflects current police practices, it may exacerbate the problem.

Machines and programs empowered with AI will also have an effect on the legal profession, as jobs that focus on data collection and research on Lexis and Westlaw will be replaced with more efficient and accurate programs. However, without general intelligence capability, much of the legal profession will still rely on human abilities, such as creativity to address new legal problems, and human compassion during the course of legal representation.

IV.   Legal and Policy Responses to Technological Innovations

The involvement of artificial intelligence in our everyday lives in 2040, especially through Big Brother-like surveillance, will raise significant issues regarding potential government abuse with the acquisition and use of large amounts of sensitive information about the general population. The current constitutional authority on technological innovations and surveillance is *Kyllo v. United States*, where the Court ruled that the Fourth Amendment protected against disruptions to practices within the privacy of the home through the use of intrusive thermal imaging equipment.[2] Relevant to the Court's analysis of whether the use of thermal imaging equipment was a search was whether the equipment was in "general public use" and whether it was used to gather details of the home that would previously be unknowable without physical intrusion.[3]

Under the Court's existing jurisprudence, surveillance of public areas in 2040 would likely pass constitutional muster. First, machines with AI capability and mood-sensing technology will be in general public use due to higher powered smartphones and other popular gadgets. Second, gathering details of activity in the public realm is not detecting private activity occurring in private areas, the search of which is protected by the Fourth Amendment's warrant requirement.[4] Thus under *Kyllo*, this type of video surveillance would not even be considered a search. Furthermore, the Court has held that the Fourth Amendment does not prohibit technology which enhances or augments sensory abilities and investigation capabilities.[5]

Although one could argue that license plates and fingerprints are exposed in the public realm and the government could manually gather the same exposed information, the techniques employed in intelligent surveillance, such as gathering and cross-referencing large amounts of surveillance data with crime databases, are arguably more invasive. The American Civil Liberties

Union ("ACLU") is one of foremost advocates for privacy rights and civil liberties in general, and has put forth a persuasive argument against license plate scanners:

> As we said at the time as we began to get questions about the technology, we don't have any fundamental objections to the technology itself — after all, a police officer could manually phone in all the tags in a parking lot to check for unpaid tickets, and this just did the same thing in a quicker, more efficient way. Sometimes the speed and efficiency of computers does fundamentally change the nature of surveillance compared to non-computerized equivalents — as with GPS tracking, for example. Quantity can change quality.[6]

With increasingly intelligent and efficient machines in 2040, the idea of exposing oneself to the public sphere will fundamentally change, and constitutional protection of our Fourth Amendment rights should change as well to modify the weak standard under *Kyllo*. When widespread and unrelenting government surveillance can track and record non-criminal but sensitive information, such as attendance at political rallies, or at abortion and HIV clinics, the Court should broaden its "reasonable expectation of privacy" test to ensure protection of unreasonable government intrusion and storing of information that many citizens would consider private. It is also important to note that the harms presented by surveillance in 2040 implicate First Amendment concerns and would likely have a chilling effect on freedom of speech and association.

If intelligent surveillance in 2040 is dominated by the private sector, this would place most harmful surveillance outside of applicable constitutional protections under the state action doctrine.[7] Problematically, the Court has allowed private conduct to play a role in defining the Fourth Amendment, and held that when a private actor invades an individual's reasonable expectation of privacy, the government may subsequently do so as well, at least to the extent the private actor already has.[8] In determining whether citizens have a reasonable expectation of privacy, the Court should not look to citizens' willingness to subject themselves to private surveillance. The private feasibility or practicality of an intrusive action should not supplant the Court's analysis of whether or not that action is constitutional.

Thus far, statutory regulation of technological communications has focused on the *acquisition* of information and collection of evidence in the Stored Communications Act ("SCA")[9] and the Wiretap Act.[10] Focusing on *when* the government can acquire information, rather than on *what* the government can or cannot do with the collected data leaves room open for unreasonable government intrusion into privacy and potential abuse, and the future regulatory response to new technology should seek to fill this gap. Ultimately, the extent to which new technology changes the conditions of our environment should be reflected in our laws and policies to ensure that our society can reap the benefits of advanced technology without sacrificing crucial rights and liberties that are central to the U.S Constitution.

---

[1] Siri. Your wish is its command, Apple Website,
http://www.apple.com/iphone/features/siri.html.

[2] Kyllo v. United States, 533 U.S 27 (2001), p. 317.

[3] *Id.*

[4] Kyllo at p. 316. "What a person knowingly exposes to the public, even in his own home of office, is not a subject of Fourth Amendment protection." Katz v. United States, 389 U.S. 347 (1967), p. 310.

[5] United States v. Knotts, 460 U.S. 276 (1983).

[6] *License Plate Scanners Logging Our Every Move*, American Civil Liberties Union Blog of Rights, Nov. 21, 2011, http://www.aclu.org/blog/tag/tracked.

[7] Textbook authors, Applying Constitutional Norms to "Private Entities," p. 203.

[8] United States v. Jacobsen, 466 U.S. 109, 117 (1984), p. 323 (upholding the search of a package previously opened by a Federal Express employee).

[9] Stored Communications and Transactional Records Access, 18 U.S.C §§2701-2709, 2711-2712, p.674-676.

[10] Interception of Wire, Oral, and Electronic Communications, 18 U.S.C §§2510 (12), p.669.

Chapter 13

The Future of Online Education, and its Enemies
Anonymous 2

If one were to even begin to imagine the future, she would need to give in to large, foundational assumptions about the evolvement of the structure of society. What will be the balance struck between civil society, economic markets, and the state? With this in mind, it is impossible to foreshadow, in light of the extreme volatility, the structure of civilization as a whole. Technological inventions can very well affect the balance of power systems (both military and economic) that now exist in the international sphere. What we can shed light on, however, is how American society may be affected by technology. No one could have predicted, for example, the invention of low power light emitting diodes replacing the incandescent filaments in light bulbs, from the standard 100 watt bulb, to an L.E.D. bulb that emits the same amount of light with less than 5watts of consumption. Similarly, communication technology will undoubtedly play an equally dramatic role. In this paper, I will focus on how communication technology will have shaped the future education.

It is difficult to imagine that the Constitution will be amended within the next 40 years. Even in these trying economic times, the will of the American people has not reached a realm where the constitutional safeguards that have been put in place, especially the actualization of the Bill of Rights within the last 50 years or so, can be safely done away with. We are, in fact, a society that is comprised of different "sub-societies," and there is no cosmopolitan cohesion that can provide for a rebirth in the American social contract within these next few decades. This does not mean, however, that the power of civil society must be anchored on existing preconceptions of the Constitution. Additionally, it also does not mean that this very same civil society cannot use technology to effectuate change within the state and the economy.

It is inevitable that the future of American education will do away with charging sky-high tuition to support the existence of traditional educational infrastructures and will move towards the facilitation of undergraduate and graduate level education through computer-based, online instruction. Not coincidentally, fiber-optic communication will play a major role in this evolvement, allowing ultra high-speed virtualization to be in every home, replacing the antiquated copper wiring that is currently providing us with Internet communication. This popular upgrade in technology will allow for anyone to be a vibrant part of the virtual classroom experience, thus making the commute from home to a dimly lit, large and impersonal classroom quite unnecessary.

This move will serve to not only allow graduates to enter the job market with very little debt so they can pursue all forms of employment, but it will also serve to give graduates the best education because they will be lectured by the very best professors in their field. No more will there be an abundance of professors teaching the same subjects. Rather, there will only be a handful of expert professors, with the rest of the educators being reduced to glorified "Teaching Assistant" positions where they will only serve to guide the student in the professor's teaching. Certainly, such a vision modifies the vast economic market that feeds off of education, such as the astronomical money that textbook publishers receive from struggling students. Furthermore, the state will be affected in that there will be a whole slew of unemployment that will exist once the physical facilities of state colleges and universities are done away with. Imagine, if you will, Iowa City without the large physical presence of the University of Iowa: This now thriving city, with its 30,000 on-campus students and more than 2,000 educators, would come to a standstill in light of the massive amount of business that depends on them. The city would undoubtedly be in for a long-term, austere period of economic transition.

Furthermore, there is the perceived danger that viewpoints will be constrained, both from the side of educators as well as from publishers. On the side of educators, there is a danger that those very few educators will teach subjects based on their political viewpoints.[1] The idea that a law professor will expose hundreds of thousands of people to a specific approach for philosophical legal construction can create a massive societal impact. Stemming from this, the specific choice of textbook from the professor can eliminate otherwise valid scholarship that will all of a sudden fail to be a shaping factor in society.

Initially, the law will respond by protecting the 'traditionalism' of institutions. In this sense, legal arguments have already been put forward that espouse learning as a largely interactive approach between students, facilitating and furthering relationships that will prepare students for the 'real world' as paramount in its importance, and that the prospect of online legal education will be a detriment in obtaining these results.[2]

Legal associations, for example, have already responded by acting as a gatekeeper to this new type of virtual legal education. The American Bar Association's guidelines that mandate that legal education be taught in a certain manner, comprising of only classroom hours in obtaining a J.D. degree that will allow the student to apply and to sit for a bar exam. This example of a private association acting as a gatekeeper to popular justice is controversial indeed.[3] After all, the ABA, in its relatively short life during the 20th century, has had its share of controversial involvements from not allowing membership of Black lawyers[4] to modern day criticisms that the ABA's policies promote high law school tuition.

To make matters worse, it is logical that the authorities of law, the professors themselves, would have no intention of changing the current educational setup of law education as it also guarantees their prominence within the current system. It is nice, no doubt, to be a big fish in a small pond, instead of being dumped into a vast sea of competition and being placed in a position where one is lower down on the food chain. It would be appropriate, then, that the future of online education have a supra-national association comprised of the public interest, one that had the power to overwrite such limitations placed by the ABA.[5]

Yet, the price being paid for the current standard of education is by the sacrifice of the mere law student, paying exorbitant prices for education that can, and will, be one day be provided by the best law professors in the field at an infinitesimal fraction of the cost, allowing law graduates to seek noble projects within society while balancing their personal lives as mothers and fathers, instead of seeking that 100+ per week law job in order to pay off that gigantic law school debt, eventually having their lives amount to nothing but a material lifestyle. However pessimistic this view is, it has plenty of merit.[6] Online education will address this problem, as the government will view it as serving a public function and consequently, the government should place limits on tuition charged by colleges and universities, both public and private, in an effort to ensure that the values of "Life, Liberty, and the Pursuit of Happiness"[7] that has been enshrined into the Constitution by the Declaration of Independence continue to survive in what will otherwise be a system of education whose means are currently constructed, whether educators choose to admit it or not, to serve only an economic interest that destroys societal values.

On the issue that online education may limit the educational viewpoint by drastically narrowing down the amount of professors that will be educating the masses, there is already a marked overabundance of politically based teaching within non-online education within schools. At the University of Iowa, for example, the legal philosophy espoused by many professors is that of legal formalism, where a student who attempts to break away from legal theory sympathetic to largely liberal idealism, into a world of legal realism that proceeds to address issues of public policy, is severely punished, academically at least, for his thoughts.[8] It is not, after all, that a student is using profanity in the classroom, for perhaps there would be a legal question to be answered[9], but here the professors of law have in large part succeeded in removing from practice those who share other politically based viewpoints of the law.[10], [11]

In looking to the future, the availability of online schools will give the student a choice of learning subjects like the law without worrying about having to follow narrow career choices on account of debt. Professors will be able to discuss the law not in a single-minded, robotic regurgitation that dates back to the days of Christopher Langdell, but rather in a manner that allows for all legal philosophies to be taught.

There is no doubt that in the future state universities and colleges will teach online and bring affordable education to the masses. It will be a responsibility of the law, educational practitioners, and legislators, however, to make sure that such education will not be blocked by the self-serving interests of those who aim to profit the most from the educational industry.

[1] See for example, Epstein, Richard, A., "Legal Education and the Politics of Exclusion", Stanford Law Review, Vol.45, No. 6, (1993), at 1607.

[2] See for example, the US News and World Report's discussion of online legal education: Burnsed, Brian, "Online Law Schools Have Yet to Pass the Bar," March 23, 2011, available at http://www.usnews.com/education/online-education/articles/2011/03/23/online-law-schools-have-yet-to-pass-the-bar

[3] See as a comparison between the public and private distinction, the discussion of centralized standard setting bodies in p. 169 of the textbook, specifically the discussion of how the Internet would have been different if AT&T had acquired its ownership.

[4] See Matzko, John, "'The Best Men of the Bar': The Founding of the American Bar Association," in The New High Priests: Lawyers in Post-Civil War America, Gerard W. Gawalt (ed.), (Westport, Conn.: Greenwood Press, 1984), pp. 75-96.

[5] See as an example of a supranational intervention, *Lawrence Lessig, The Spam Wars*, found on page 176, where he discusses the dispute between MIT and ORBS, where ORBS, through its authority, restricted the email communication of MIT. This authority was then surpassed and overturned by BC Tel, who had supervisory control of ORBS.

[6] See for example, Dershowitz, Alan, "Letters to a Young Lawyer," a book that discusses the pivotal turns that define a young lawyer's career path, and the permanency of those choices.

[7] See, "Applying Constitutional Norms to Private Entities," on page 203 of textbook, where the "state action doctrine" is discussed by seeing if a) the institution is serving a public function, and b) whether the point of contact between government and the private party is sufficient to impose constitutional constraints. In the case of education, there is a public interest in ensuring that those who graduate can pursue a life in their chosen path.

[8] In essence, legal education in the formalist tradition has failed to 'Foster a Tolerant Society' by failing to protect the student's freedom of expression, especially those views that refuse to believe that a theoretical foundation can support the entirety of legal thinking. (See page 532 of text)

[9] See FCC v. Pacifica, where time, place, and manner restrictions were placed on George Carlin's comedy routine that was broadcast on the airwaves.

[10] See for example, Jeremy Waldron's discussion on "Law and Disagreement."

[11] "No man may be prevented from saying or publishing what he thinks, or from refusing in his speech or other utterances to give equal weight to the views of his opponents." *Red Lion Broadcasting v. FCC*, Textbook, page 208, where Justice White delivers the majority opinion.

Chapter 14

How Technology Will Shape the Next Thirty Years
Anonymous 3

    The past twenty years has undoubtedly seen some prolific advancements in technology. Televisions are getting to be as thin as a deck of cards. Intel seemingly adds a new core to their microchips every year. Many popular mobile phones no longer have buttons. "Smaller, faster, and more powerful" has become the mantra for the likes of Google, Apple, Sony, Motorola, and LG. As technology continues to advance, our appliances, televisions, and mobile phones will only get thinner and more powerful. If a product does not already have some sort of microchip it will. More and more products will connect to the internet via a high speed WIFI connection. In short, if I were to sum up theme for the technological revolution in two words, they would be "smaller and connected."

    No single device has seen more development in the past ten years than the mobile phone. I cannot even imagine where mobile phones will be in the next thirty years. I predict that people will come to rely on their phones even more than they do now. Samsung and Motorola have started integrating NFC chips into their mobile phones.[1] These phones, which utilize Android OS, essentially function as a credit card because users can scan their phones on a NFC compatible device and log purchases on their respective credit card accounts. Although the overwhelming majority of phones do not have Google Wallet or NFC chips, it is likely that more phones will integrate these features in the future. People may be hesitant to use their phones as credit cards at first, but most will probably come around when the technology becomes more safe and secure. Google Wallet is just one example of how the mobile phone has infiltrated various aspects of our everyday life. As phones become more powerful, it is likely that phones will infiltrate other aspects of our life.

    As much as advanced mobile phones have benefitted our lives, these advancements do present some issues worth discussing. Importantly, as people become more reliant on their mobile phones, the more personal information they will relinquish to third parties. For instance, most new smartphones sold in the United States contain GPS chips which enable users to easily navigate their city. Earlier this year, intrepid researchers exposed a "bug" within iPhones which caused the phone to secretly track its user's location.[2] Many iPhone users were understandably upset upon learning about this hidden feature. Richard H. Thaler, a writer for the *New York Times*, responded to this controversy by proposing a new privacy standard for storing personal data: "If a business collects data on consumer electronically, it should provide them with a version of that data that is easy to download and export to another website. Think of it this way: you have lent the company your data, and you'd like a copy for your own use."[3]   Other writers responded in a completely different fashion, including CNET writer Larry Downes. Downes, who apparently does not mind if his phone tracks him: "By and large, however, most of the information still sits in increasingly crowded data warehouses, doing next to nothing. In the best-case scenario, it is being used responsibly by those we interact with to improve future interactions through customization, recommendations, promotional pricing, more relevant advertising, better customer service, and more-focused product design."[4]

Downes may be right. The more I use Google Chrome, the more efficient it becomes. It learns my personal information so I do not need to repeatedly input my address and credit card information every time I make an online purchase. My life is better because Google Chrome strives to be more efficient. However, despite the seemingly good intentions of Google and Apple, there must be some kind of regulatory system that prevents companies from misusing this information. As with other cyber law issues, there are various means to regulate companies such as Google, Apple, and Facebook, including governmental regulation, market regulation, and self-regulation.[5] Even though a Facebook user's personal information might just "sit in a crowded data warehouse,"   it still remains available to Facebook or third parties who are willing to pay the price to access it. Self-regulation simply cannot remain a viable option for these companies because they will find new and creative ways to log a user's information without his or her knowledge. Apple claimed that iPhones were tracking their users because of faulty software,[6] but that seems rather disingenuous, especially since Apple spends years meticulously crafting its software and hardware. Market regulation is not necessarily a viable option because Google, Apple, and Facebook control much of the mobile device and digital marketplace. Even after "Antennagate"[7] and the GPS tracking controversy, Apple will still sell millions of iPhones every year.[8]

As a result, governmental regulation might be the best means to govern the manner in which these companies handle a user's personal information. Thaler's *NY Times* article provides guidance on how the government could regulate the way companies handle personal information.[9] Using the iPhone as an example, the government could require Apple to inform iPhone users when their phone logs personal information or current location. It might even be useful for Apple to create an application that details how the phone and various applications have handled the user's personal information. One way or another, the user should be involved in how companies handle his information. If the Facebook iPhone application randomly tracks his location, the user should be able to both know about it and opt out of tracking. Under this hypothetical legislation, the user should always know how companies handle his information and should have the ability to protect himself by preventing the dissemination of that information when necessary.

A primary reason for giving the user more control over how companies handle his information is to protect the user from hackers. Earlier this year, hackers attacked Sony Online Entertainment and accessed the account information of the 24.6 million SOE users.[10] These hackers may have stolen more than 20,000 credit card and bank account numbers.[11] Undoubtedly, Sony can enhance their server security in order to prevent future attacks. However, another means to protect the user involves giving the user control over what information Sony stores on their servers. As a user of Sony Playstation's online services, I would appreciate the ability to prevent Sony from storing my credit card information after I purchase digital goods in their online store, especially after the recent hacking fiasco. Once I gave Sony my credit card information, I could not erase it from their servers. There should be laws in place which give me that ability so I can protect myself from rogue hackers.

As the hacking community continues to grow, it is becoming increasingly more apparent that hackers can seriously threaten the well-being of the entire country. Currently, Anonymous is one of the biggest and most influential hacking group. The next thirty years will not only see major advancements in technology, but will also see the creation of groups similar to Anonymous, or possibly even worse ones that are motivated solely by anarchy. Anonymous has yet to launch a full-scale terrorist attack, but one cannot doubt its ability to do so. Instead, Anonymous has engaged in smaller attacks on controversial institutions, such as the Westboro Baptist Church, Church of Scientology, and even a Mexican drug cartel.[12]

It is easy to trust that Anonymous has our best interests at heart because it is going after the likes of a Mexican drug cartel. This trust is, however, fragile. Suppose Americans elect a president that Anonymous finds both distasteful and untrustworthy. What happens when Anonymous or a similar group launches cyber attacks against public utilities in protest? It is certainly possible. In fact, an unknown organization recently hacked into the control system of the city water utility in Springfield, Illinois.[13] The hackers apparently launched their attack from IP addresses in Russia and accessed the system.[14] Once inside, the hackers remotely turned the system on and off, which caused the pump to burn out.[15] In examining this hack, Joe Weiss of Applied Control Solution stated the obvious: "there very easily could be other utilities as we speak who have their networks compromised."

This type of vulnerability not only demonstrates the power that these hackers can wield, but also provides an indication of how the next terrorist regime will attack the United States. If hackers can remotely access a city water station with ease, what will stop them from accessing our nuclear power plants? There must be laws in place that mandate all major utilities throughout the nation undertake serious measures to prevent such attacks. Every back alley into a system must be impeded at all costs. For the most important utilities such as nuclear power plants, the Department of Homeland Security may consider creating a specialized task force dedicated towards securing nuclear power plants from cyber attacks. The Department of Homeland Security created the TSA shortly after 9/11. We cannot wait for another 9/11 to justify creating this special force. It should happen before terrorists hack into our nuclear power plants and cause catastrophic destruction.

Regulating the hacking organizations during the next thirty years will prove to be difficult. Currently, the Computer Fraud and Abuse Act provides a means through which the government can prosecute hackers for knowingly accessing a computer without authorization or exceeding authorized access.[16] The federal government would certainly benefit from updating the Computer Fraud and Abuse Act or even creating a whole new legal scheme to regulate hacking since the Computer Fraud and Abuse Act is rather outdated. The key to an effective new legal scheme involves incorporating stiff penalties for repeated hacking and for large scale hacking. This may deter hackers. However, as the art of hacking develops, the savvier these hackers become at disguising their identity. Even if the government manages to arrest members of Anonymous, the group will still survive.[17] This is a global group that wields tremendous power. The most effective form of regulation, however, may be private regulation. Perhaps a group such as Anonymous can serve as the "watch dog" for purely anarchist hackers who have no moral compass.

If they prove to be trustworthy, Anonymous can play the role that Media3 did in *Media3 Technologies v. Mail Abuse Prevention System.*[18] Media3 is a "web-hosting" company that enforces the standard industry practice of requiring its customers to sign an Acceptable Use Policy for conducting business, which includes an "anti-spam" provision that prohibits its users from directly or indirectly spamming innocent internet users.[19] Anonymous could ultimately set industry standards which govern "appropriate" and "inappropriate" hacking. Hacking in the name of social justice would fall under "appropriate" hacking, whereas hacking to cause widespread destruction would obviously qualify as "inappropriate" hacking. If a group engages in inappropriate hacking, Anonymous could go after them to limit their influence in the hacking world and prevent unjustified attacks.

Ultimately, as technology advances and as the hacking culture matures, our county must adapt. Americans should enjoy the fruits that advanced technology brings them, but should also be wary of the sacrifices this technology may require.

---

[1] See http://www.google.com/wallet/#instore-promo and
http://www.bgr.com/2011/10/24/nfc-chip-shipments-may-surpass-1-2-billion-units-by-2015/
[2] "Your iPhone's Watching You. Should you Care?" http://news.cnet.com/8301-13579_3-20055885-37.html?tag=mncol;txt
[3] "Show Us the Data (It's Ours After All)"

http://www.nytimes.com/2011/04/24/business/24view.html?_r=1

[4] "Privacy Panic Debate: Whose Data Is It?" http://news.cnet.com/8301-13578_3-20057682-38.html

[5] See Casebook, Chapter 6, pages 646-665.

[6] See "Your iPhone's Watching You" http://news.cnet.com/8301-13579_3-20055885-37.html?tag=mncol;txt

[7] "Apple's iPhone 4 Antennagate Timeline"
http://www.pcworld.com/article/201297/apples_iphone_4_antennagate_timeline.html

[8] "iPhone 4S Weekend Sales Top Four Million"
http://www.pcworld.com/article/201297/apples_iphone_4_antennagate_timeline.html

[10] "Sony Hacked Again; 25 Million Entertainmetn Users' Info at Risk"
http://www.wired.com/gamelife/2011/05/sony-online-entertainment-hack/

[11] *Id.*

[12] "Anonymous: The Secret Group's 5 Biggest Hacks"
http://theweek.com/article/index/212846/anonymous-the-secret-groups-5-biggest-hacks; "Anonymous Threat on Mexican Cartel going forward, source says

[13] "Attack on City Water Station Destroys Pump"
http://www.wired.com/threatlevel/2011/11/hackers-destroy-water-pump/

[14] *Id.*

[15] *Id.*

[16] Casebook at 734

[17] FBI Arrests 14 Hackers, But Anonymous Still Sailing & 'Seeking Shiny Booty'
http://www.networkworld.com/community/blog/fbi-arrests-14-hackers-anonymous-still-sailin

[18] Casebook at 173

[19] *Id* at 174

Chapter 15

The Ever Expanding and All Consuming Internet
Anonymous 4

I.   Introduction

There are few areas of the modern world that have not been touched by or adapted into cyberspace. Most if not all communication technology at present involves the Internet in some shape or form. Radio, television, mail, and phoning can all be done over the Internet. The introduction of Web 2.0 transformed the landscape of cyberspace as well as increased its exposure with the integration of user-generated content.[1] The Internet has become its own vast world where over 6 billion users participate in personal activities, social interactions, and commerce.[2] Users contributing to the web have ushered in a new era of norms whereby people's behaviors are changing and adapting with technology. Consolidation and efficiency is another trend of technology that has altered the behavior of the modern individual. For example, devices and gadgets are increasingly linked to the Internet and portable. This trend indicates that the Internet will be accessible everywhere, not just from personal laptops and cell phones but also from public devices. Therefore, public access to the Internet through communication devices will be made more freely available as the modern world becomes more reliant and involved with cyberspace. As real space and cyberspace collide, the question is what the future will hold in the form of regulations.

II. 2040 Forecasts: Everything and Everyone is Moving to the Internet

Cyberspace has become the most pervasive piece of technology ever to exist and the future holds that it will continue to make other competing devices obsolete. Commerce has been a driving force behind the development and expansion of the Internet since its inception. However, as trade and development "go online" the future holds that aspects of real space regulations will need to change in order to adapt to the nebulous World Wide Web.

A.   Online Trade & Commerce

Reflecting on the number of Internet users at present, thirty years from now cyberspace will include some form of online interaction with almost everyone on the planet. People will continue to become more involved with the Internet, spending more time online than functioning in the real world. For this reason businesses are adapting to online buying, and at the same time changing consumer behaviors. Businesses are using the Internet as a tool. The tool is not only used to effectively sell products but more importantly to gain information on individuals for future sales.[3] As a result, in the future, consumers will have a completely tailored experience leading to an expansion of trade and commerce. Since the Internet is dominated by private businesses, the regulations will be bottom-up as technology is driven and developed by commerce. Companies will want to continue with online trade and as a result will want to keep customers protected from fraud or security breaches. The ability of private entities to enforce rules, and the inflexibility of real space laws in cyberspace, might engender overarching trade practices in the future, driven by technology.

B. Cloud Computing Systems

As the Internet accumulates more information and users, cloud computing will become essential in cyberspace. Cloud computing is used in a variety of ways by both individuals and large and small businesses.[4] In thirty years, all information and forms of media will be digitized and accessible through the Internet. The modern world has become increasingly mobile and the ability to access information at any one point in time and at any given location will become the norm. As the demand for instant access increases among the Internet's billions of users, and everything moves from the physical world to the digital, cloud systems will be heavily relied upon to provide content. However, as more businesses turn to cloud computing, the landscape of the IT service industry will vastly change and experience heavy downsizing.[5] Also, the demand for actual software will change, as cloud applications that can be accessed anywhere provide more user friendly options at lower costs.[6] Cloud Computing systems will have to become more versatile in the future as technology continues to make advancements, and the demand for mobility, speed, and access increases.

II.   Changing Social Behavior and Interactions

Use of the Internet and more specifically social networking, has opened the gateway to a dichotomy of online behavior. Users of cyberspace are divided into people who want to remain anonymous and those who want to be visible. As technology advances and social networking changes and expands, the ability to remain anonymous will no longer exist. Since much of human interaction involves exchanges over the Internet, the push towards having an identity or presence in cyberspace will become essential within society. Choosing not to participate in the online world would be equivalent to never stepping foot outside one's home. Even today we experience physical human interaction becoming replaced by cyber connections, forming friends, relationships, and communities online. The extent to which human interaction will survive is questionable. The future holds a dark and dangerous path as social behavior is molded by technology.

III.   Regulating the Internet

Thirty years from now, when everyone is on the Internet participating, acting, and working, what kind of controls will be in place and who will regulate those controls? A hybrid authority will manifest with a part bottom-up regulation from the private sector and part top-down enforcement from the government.[7] In the future, a balanced form of regulation will be constructed in order to protect consumers from monopolies and at the same time from Orwellian control.

A. A Layer of Code

The one fact about the Internet that can be relied upon is that cyberspace is not static, will never be static, and is always changing. In the past, the architecture of the Internet made it difficult to regulate because of the inability to authenticate users' identities.[8] The Internet has been able to overcome this with the development of TCP/IPs and cookies.[9] IP addresses and cookies have revolutionized the ability to authenticate, identify, and trace individuals who use the Internet.[10] Recently the information from IPs and cookies allow for remarketing—targeted advertising from gleaning browser information—and geolocating to occur.[11] As forms of communications increasingly become involved with cyberspace and as the Internet changes to reveal more information about users, regulations will be more adaptable and possible. Lawrence Lessig describes future regulation to include architectures of control, layering onto interactions on the Web in order to correct or eliminate imperfections. One of the answers that Lessig promotes is the use of code.[12] The government regulates the Internet not in a direct manner but with indirect methods using current technology. For instance, the government asks for data collected through intermediaries or private companies in order to conduct investigations.[13] Since this is a trend set by advancements in technology, the government could utilize code to regulate the Internet. In the future, the government will use technology integrated from private companies in order to enforce laws.

B. Protecting Privacy

Privacy protection is a concern that will always be an issue when regulating the Internet. The Internet is the one place where accessing another person's information or restricted information is highly possible. However, regulating the Internet and providing privacy protection might limit the inherent freedoms that the online world affords. In the future, the Internet should have privacy protection standards that are applied bottom-up, but more importantly enforced top-down.

A method that will be developed in the future is the ability to have identifying markers in order to navigate the Internet. Lessig proposes a layer of code provided as a form of identity termed Privacy Enhancing Technology (PET).[14]

> PET . . . would enable individuals to more effectively control the data about them that they reveal. It would also enable individuals to have a trustable pseudonymous identity that websites and others should be happy to accept. Thus, with this technology, if a site needs to know I am over 18, or an American citizen, or authorized to access a university library, the technology can certify this data without revealing anything else. Of all the changes to information practices that we could imagine, this would be the most significant in reducing the extent of redundant or unnecessary data flowing in the ether of the network[15]

The probability that thirty years in the future layers of code will be used to regulate privacy grows increasingly high as more people conduct their lives online. Security breaches are a constant threat and technology should be used to combat potentially dangerous exposure or illegal actions without limiting the inherent freedom of the average Internet user.

IV.   Net Neutrality

The outcome of net neutrality, or more specifically the conservation of equal access, will determine the landscape of cyberspace in the future.[16] Online companies describe the potential changeover to limited access as "the equivalent of having the toaster pay for the ability to plug itself into the electrical grid."[17] Ever since the U.S. Court of Appeals decision overruled the FCC's authority over broadband, net neutrality remains in a precarious position.[18] However, another government agency, like the FTC, could potentially protect net neutrality from being eliminated by corporations like Comcast.[19] If authority is not given to the FTC, net neutrality will remain unprotected from private controls, because the government is hesitant to enact laws that would completely alter the conditions of a vital economic vehicle, and also because the potential limitations on technological development would be devastating.[20]

V.   Changing the Law

As the development and expansion of the Internet causes changes in social norms and behaviors, so too will laws cause change, when they are developed to respond to the needs of regulating an open, expanding, and unrestricted cyberspace. Also, adaptation is a common motif in today's world and the law will likely follow the same into the future as cyberspace becomes the dominant place where legal transactions and social interactions occur.

Popular culture likens cyberspace to the Wild West, a frontier where the law of the land is ambiguous and not consistently enforced.[21] However, the future of the Internet will encounter an increase in top-down regulation and enforcement. Instead of the constitutional reform that Lessig advocates, administrative agencies will be empowered to lay down the law of the land. Government agencies will be given more plenary authority to regulate certain sections or aspects of the online world that come under their purview. Legislation like the Computer Fraud and Abuse Act, or the Espionage Act, will be amended to directly address a changed world in 2040. While bottom-up regulation is currently adaptable, the powers of private companies are limited to functionality within cyberspace and have no real legal authority. In the future the Government will provide increasing regulatory enforcement, gradually changing the norms of users and entities on the Internet.

VI.   Conclusion

Thirty years from now the Internet will be the place where most human interaction take place, changing facets of commercial exchange and social interaction. As a result regulation is necessary and will be from both the private and public sectors. Technical advances in code will help place a layer of regulation onto online activity in order to give users security. Bottom-up and Top-down forms of regulation will work together in layers to protect user welfare without taking away the integral freedoms that the Internet provides.

---

[1] Web 2.0, http://en.wikipedia.org/wiki/Web_2.0.

[2] Internet Usage Statistics *available at*
http://www.Internetworldstats.com/stats.htm.

[3] Google Ad Innovations: Remarketing *available at*
http://www.google.com/ads/innovations/remarketing.html.

[4] John Bussey, Seeking Safety in Clouds, Wall Street Journal, available at
http://online.wsj.com/article/SB10001424053111904060604576572930344327162.htm
l?KEYWORDS=cloud+computing.

[5] *Id.*

[6] *Id.*

[7] Richard A. Spinello, Cyberethics: Morality and Law in Cyberspace, 49 (2011).

[8] Lawrence Lessig, Code Version 2.0, 43-47 (2006).

[9] *Id.*

[10] *Id.*

[11] *Id.*

[12] *Id.*

[13] *Id.*

[14] Lawrence Lessig, Code Version 2.0, 226 (2006).

[15] *Id.*

[16] Times Topic: Net Neutrality *available at*
http://topics.nytimes.com/topics/reference/timestopics/subjects/n/net_neutrality/in
dex.html?offset=15&s=newest.

[17] *Id.*

[18] *Id.*

[19] *Id.*

[20] Release, FTC Issues Staff Report on Broadband Connectivity Competition Policy Report Urges Caution on Network Neutrality Regulation, June 27, 2007, *available at*
http://www.ftc.gov/opa/2007/06/broadband.shtm.

[21] Times Topic: Net Neutrality *available at*
http://topics.nytimes.com/topics/reference/timestopics/subjects/n/net_neutrality/in
dex.html?offset=15&s=newest.

Chapter 16

The Future of Computing:
Invisible, Embedded, and Ubiquitous
Anonymous 5

The year depicted is 2054, and in this future criminals are caught before the crimes they commit. This is the plot that drives the film *Minority Report*, but one of the more memorable aspects of the film does not come in the form of the protagonist, John Anderton, preventing future crime, but in the way in which advertising is able to locate and target individuals with messages specifically tailored to their needs.

In one striking scene,[1] John Anderton, on the lam for a crime he did not (yet) commit, is frantically moving through a shopping mall. As he moves about we can see a green laser scan his retina and suddenly he is bombarded with virtual billboards and 3-D digital sprites calling his name and offering him products and services—"John Anderton, you could use a Guinness" (yes, he could). Mr. Anderton is accustomed to this world and he continues without paying attention to the advertisements, but to the viewer in the present day the scene is overwhelming.

What we see in this scene is the seamless integration of computing ability and information technology with everyday life. The technology depicted in the scene is an accurate depiction of the future, and in fact the trend towards this environment has already begun. This essay will examine the possibility of this technological landscape, technological trends that are pointing us to that future, the problems they could create, and how the law will deal with those problems.

I.   The Future Landscape

The technology that allows the world of *Minority Report* to function already has a name in the present day, in fact it has several names—"Ambient Intelligence," "The Internet of Things," or "Ubiquitous, Pervasive, Proactive and Automatic Computing" (referred to from here on, for this paper, as "AmI").[2] While there are several denominations, the vision is the same. The future will see the computer leave the box, becoming embedded in the physical world and receding into the background. They will be everywhere and will be utilized in every function of every day life. The Internet, in the shape of a network of computers limited in output by certain devices, will transform and include miniaturized computer devices that are embedded in everyday objects that constantly communicate to create a sensitive, responsive, intelligent, and interactive network.[3] This will create a technological environment that moves with us and is attuned to our senses, adaptive to our needs, and always one step ahead.[4] Imagine a future where sensors in our clothes--or even in our bodies--

will be able to tell our temperature, heart rate, breathing pattern and communicate with devices to adjust the environment accordingly. Or consider sensors that will be able to detect our movements and pace relative to products and gauge our interest in them. If we move past something quick, yet our purchasing history indicates we might be interested in that object, then an advertisement might pop up and alert us visually or aurally. The advertisement would be discrete, only for the individual to hear, but it would also be smart and sensitive in that it would be able to detect if a person is even in a shopping "mood".

II.   Where We are Today

There are many technological trends today that make this future realistic. First, we are already witnessing the computer "leaving the box". During the last ten years the computer has been merging with cell phone. The computer is leaving the desktop and going into our pockets. These new devices are always on, always connected, and carry our personal details. These devices not only track and store information about how they are used (in the form of cookies) but they also keep track of where they (you) have been. These two types of data derived from the mobile phone can then be processed and aggregated to map a user's behavior and preferences.

Second, cameras are everywhere. They are on our phones, our computers, and on the walls of libraries, convenience stores, stadiums, apartment lobbies, buses, street corners and schools. In London alone it is estimated that there are as many as 4.2 million closed circuit television cameras, and that the average Londoner is photographed over 300 times per day.[5] Our location and movement cannot only be tracked by the device we carry in our pockets, but by the face we wear. Throughout Europe and the USA, facial recognition software in cameras has been used for security for sporting events, border control, and casinos.[6]

Third, RFID (radio frequency identification) allows for chips smaller than a grain of sand to transmit information stored on the chip to a nearby RFID reader. RFID's are already widely used, often on an inanimate object, like a highway tollbooth "EZ Pass", or passport, or shipping container.[7] However, recently chips have been embedded in animals to help retrieve them if they become lost, and this practice could be extended to humans. RFID makes it possible to attach a unique identifying code to every object in the world. The use of a unique identification system could create a global registration system where every physical object is identified and could be linked to its owner or purchaser.[8]

Finally, the barrier between the physical identity and digital identity is slowly becoming inextricable. Different aspects of one's personality are being reduced to bytes, run through algorithms and turned into data.[9]

In sum, we are trending toward AmI. Over time, devices will get smaller and smarter. To the extent they blend in and are one step ahead of us, there will be an increase in the production and exchange of personal information. And with the possibility that everything will be networked, the line between physical world and digital world will be more difficult to distinguish.

III.   Problems and Issues

A. Privacy

In the future world of Ambient Intelligence, the privacy problems created during the Internet Age[10] will transfer from the cyber world to the physical world. The Internet provided that each action taken by a user could be tracked and logged. Each online activity creates trail of information left by the user. Details like what sites have been visited, what content was viewed, and for how long. The collection of this information is effortless. Moreover, due to the effortless nature of the online data-collection, the practice does not carry over into the physical world, as acquiring the same amount of information would require immense resources.[11] However, in the future world of AmI, where computer devices are seamless, embedded, and ubiquitous, the loss of privacy that traditionally occurred online will continue into the physical world. If all products have the future equivalent of an RFID chip, then not only can the retailer track the life of the good after it has been transferred to the purchaser, the retailer will know when it is used, for how long, and if it returns to the point of sale.

B. Government Surveillance

When data-collection practices of the online world spill over into physical world, what comes to mind are images of a society conditioned by constant asymmetrical surveillance. There is a justified fear of pervasive government surveillance in the world of AmI. The Fourth Amendment provides protection against "unreasonable searches and seizures," and requires probable cause to support each warrant issued. In *Katz v. United States*[12] the Supreme Court found an improper warrantless search because the defendant had a reasonable expectation of privacy which society was prepared to consider reasonable. Later in *Kyllo v. United States*[13] the Supreme Court applied *Katz* and held that there was a reasonable expectation of privacy in that the technology used was not in common use and allowed the government to obtain information that was otherwise unattainable without physical entry. Therefore, the "reasonable expectation of privacy" has an inverse relationship with technologies in common use. In the AmI world, tracking equipment will be ubiquitous and therefore a *Kyllo* "reasonable expectation of privacy" cannot exist vis-à-vis the AmI system.

C. Enclosing the Public Sphere[14]

Location and architecture can undermine accessibility to areas generally considered public.[15] AmI allows for a more sophisticated and layered access control. If every object is networked by some equivalent of RFID it then becomes possible to restrict access to areas according to certain dislikes or demographics.[16] Sensors will be able to tell what kind of clothes a person is wearing, whether that person is sick, or has a criminal record, bad credit, or is linked to a movement to which the property owners are opposed.[17]

IV.   The Law's Response

A. Response to Privacy

One solution to the problem of privacy in AmI is to have federal statutory requirement that personal data collected in the course of any interaction may only be used to complete that interaction.[18]   Another option, which is end user regulation, is to allow a person to use a devise that would be the equivalent of a privacy-cloaking device. This would allow those who have an expectation of privacy, whether persistent or ad-hoc, to be in public with a greater degree of anonymity.

B. Response to Surveillance

In order to increase accountability of invisible surveillance, a law should be enacted to require legally enforceable access to information relating to identity and the ability to correct any mistakes.[19]

In order to protect against government surveillance the "reasonable expectation" standard should be abandoned and replaced with a framework that takes into account the harms caused by surveillance balanced against state interest.[20]

C. Response to Enclosure

In order to maintain the public sphere, states could adopt, as California has,[21] state constitutional provisions protecting reasonable access to privately owned centers open to the general public.

V.   Conclusion

Fifty years ago, a computer took up an entire room. Today they are many times more powerful and fit in a pocket. We are moving toward computing that will be invisible, embedded and ubiquitous. The legal world is going to have to adapt in many ways, as it is likely that underlying assumptions on which the law has relied will be upended. As new legal boundaries are drawn, society will have to readjust its baseline expectations with respect privacy, surveillance and open access.

---

[1] http://www.youtube.com/watch?v=oBaiKsYUdvg

[2] Andrade, *Future Trends In The Regulation Of Personal Identity And Legal Personification In The Context Of Ambient Intelligence Environment*, The Law of The Future and The Future of Law, 2011, pg. 567.

[3] Id 570

[4] Id 570

[5] Kevin Werbach, *Sensors and Sensibility*, 28 Cardozo L. Rev. 2321

[6] http://en.wikipedia.org/wiki/Facial_recognition_system#Notable_users_and_deployments

[7] Kevin Werbach, *Sensors and Sensibility*, 28 Cardozo L. Rev. 2321

[8] https://www.privacyrights.org/ar/RFIDposition.htm

[9] Id, Andrade, page 571

[10] Present day

[11] Jerry Kang, *Information Privacy in Cyber Space*, 50 Stan. L. Rev. 1193

[12] Katz v. United States 389 U.S. 347

[13] Kyllo V. Untied States 533 U.S. 27

[14] Jerry Kang, *Pervausive Computing: Embedding the Public Sphere*, 62 Wash. & Lee Rev. 122 2005

[15] A park, market, or library that is not located on a bus route or is separated from a segment of the community by an interstate highway.

[16] Jerry Kang, *Pervausive Computing: Embedding the Public Sphere*, 62 Wash. & Lee Rev. 122 2005

[17] Private property owners are generally allowed to exclude speech on their own property. In Hudgens v. NLRB 424 U.S. 507 the Supreme Court ruled that malls, as private entities, are not subject to First Amendment norms.

[18] This is known as the rule of "functionally necessary use," which was originally a rule applied in cyber space limiting how information could be used after a transaction. See Kang, supra note 18, at 135

[19] This could be an enactment that mirrors the "Fair Information Practices" for information systems proposed in the 1973 HEW Report, see Cyberlaw text book, page 646.

[20] Daniel Solove, *A Taxonomy of Privacy*, University of Pennsylvania Law Review, Jan. 2006 Vol 154, 447.

[21] In Pruneyard Shopping Center v. Robins, 447 U.S. 74, the Supreme Court upheld California's state constitutional provision protecting leafleting in a private mall.